WASHED

IN THE

BLOOD

WASHED IN THE BLOOD

SHELTON L. WILLIAMS

ZONE PRESS
Denton, Texas

WASHED IN THE BLOOD
Shelton L. Williams

SECOND EDITION

Published in the United States of America
By Zone Press
an imprint of Rogers Publishing and Consulting, Inc.
201 North Austin
Denton, Texas 76201
info@zonepress.com

Editing and Design: Jim O. Rogers
Photography: Dan Setterberg and Shel Hershorn
Art: Mike King
Copy edit: Charlotte Beckham

ISBN: 0-9777558-6-X

Judge, there is enough ignorance in Odessa, Texas to justify an eight-year institution!

Warren Burnett, explaining the need for a four-year university in Odessa.

v

WASHED IN THE BLOOD

CHAPTER 1
The Stock Pond

The crisp air of a West Texas night in early spring is distinctive. The breeze is gentle and not yet erratic or even dangerous as it becomes later in "tornado season." The stars, millions of them, seem near enough to touch. It's the smell. No matter how beautiful it is, no matter how still the breeze, the smell of crude oil is still there. You might forget what pure air smells like but on certain nights and at certain times, that odor will hit you and remind you that things just aren't as pure as you think. March 21, 1961, was just such a night.

Betty Williams and Mack Herring noticed the smell but neither commented on it. Might be that they didn't really smell it but chances are they did and just didn't say anything. They had other things to think about. Mack's jeep had sped over the oilfield roads taking every bump hard as they drove in silence to the stock pond. Betty, sitting there in her pink baby doll pajamas and duster, had shivered in the cold. Now they were at the pond. The smell of cows intermingled with the crude to make the place a pungent reminder that West Texas really was out in the middle of nowhere.

Mack had helped Betty from the jeep and had retrieved his Red football jacket with the white leather sleeves. She had never worn it before even when they going together. He had not wanted anyone to know they were seeing each other secretly. She was reluctant to give it back to him now, but then she also did not want to chance ruining it. As they chatted briefly about the right spot to go, the clouds moved more quickly above, as if the gods wanted to move them just to have a little bit better view. Mack had to go back to the jeep once to get the string of wire and weights that he had gotten from the Odessa American newspaper. There had been just too much to carry in one trip. Betty, usually talkative to a fault, had stood silently as he made the trip.

When he came back, he asked her how she was. Fine, she said, fine. "OK, "he said, should I spread this blanket?" "Oh, no, that's not necessary," she said. With that, he smoothed out the ground next to the pond and rid it of any rocks or mesquite twigs that might have gathered there. "Kneel down," he said. "No, wait, Mack. I want a kiss. You said we could kiss." "Yes, OK," he said. He held her by the shoulders and tried to give her a simple kiss on the lips. She parted her lips and drew him in to a longer kiss with their tongues intermingling. He broke it off too quickly. "OK, kneel down," he said. Slowly, sliding her hands on his jeans as she went down, she knelt. Mack picked up his 12-gauge and held it to her temple. "Tell me when you are ready," Mack said. "Now," she said. Mack then pulled the trigger of the 12-gauge and blew off the back third of Betty's head.

The location where Betty Williams died is today
known as "Dead Girl's Pond"

--Dan Setterberg

CHAPTER II
Baseball Practice

Baseball is a lesser sport in West Texas. Football is King. In West Texas high school football is the King of Kings. In Odessa, kids grew up hearing stories of Byron Townsend, Karl Schlemeyer and Hayden Fry. No matter how good they were or what sacrifices they were willing to make, they would never be as good as those guys. They could never run as fast, tackle as hard, or endure as much pain as the high school legends before them. If they were to be real men, they would play football and perhaps have the opportunity to play on the same practice field as Ronnie Goodwin. They just could never be as great. Other sports--track, tennis, or baseball—were passable diversions, but they fell well below football. Even the final spring training intra-squad scrimmages drew larger audiences than championship baseball games. Baseball is a lesser sport.

But in March 1961 it was baseball season. I played and loved baseball. In a perfect world I would be big enough and have a strong enough arm to play pro ball. In the real world, I was a fairly solid hitter and an average position player, no matter which position the coach chose. As a junior, I would not get to play much, but Coach Cook wanted my bat in the line-up somewhere. I had occasional power, and no one could remember when I hadn't hit at least .300.

But where to put me? In football, my second favorite sport, I was a natural middle guard in the Permian High School system. Stout, quick, disciplined, and determined, I would foolishly stick my nose into anything. I broke five Rydell helmets my senior year. But in baseball my junior year, I had no natural position yet, and Cook had all-star seniors everywhere he looked—except left field. When Gary Crain, senior All State fullback with a scholarship to the University of Texas, was scheduled to pitch, perhaps, Cook thought, I could take Crain's position in left field.

The wind blows hard in West Texas in March. No trees slow it down. No tall buildings arrest its movement. It just blows. Flight patterns of fly balls hit into the West Texas sky sometimes look like drunken bumble bees, sometimes like darts. At least that was my experience on March 22, 1961. As Cook fungoed ball after ball my way, only the occasional one accidentally hit my glove and none of them stuck. Mounting frustration made me field even worse. I even began to fumble ground balls. I was on the verge of tears when the strangest thing happened. My mother walked out onto the field. Frustration gave way to embarrassment as my chubby little mom in a flowered dress talked with Cook and looked towards me. "Mama, what in the hell are you doin'?" I thought. Cook looked my way and then gestured me in from the field. Twenty other baseball players stopped whatever drill they were doing to watch me trot in. No one could ever remember a mom on a ball field, not even a baseball field.

"Mama, what's goin' on?" I asked. She was in tears. Cook, who had not a sensitive bone in his former Marine's body, walked away so my mom and I could speak alone. But she could not speak. She was overcome by emotion. She clutched at me, cried, and tried to utter a word without success. "Mama, calm down. What is it? Are you OK? Is Daddy OK?" At the mention of my father's name, she got control. "Shelly," she said, "They have killed Betty!" I could not take it in. My cousin went to school across town, the old Odessa High School, OHS. Mention of her name did not belong at Permian.

12

She had no connection to baseball. "Betty who?" I said. "Betty who?" "Betty Williams," she blurted, Betty Williams!"

"Betty's dead?" I stammered. That could not be. Not that the thought of death and Betty were inseparable. She had mentioned it frequently. She wanted to die, she said. Dying was preferable to life, especially in West Texas, she said. She had tried to kill herself before, once with four aspirin. She was not called "Drama Mama" just for being the star in three OHS stage productions her junior year. Everything was drama with Betty. But every time she had ever talked of death with me as we sat in our family's '53 Oldsmobile out in front of my house or hers—every time—we had ended up making out. She was dead? "They" killed her? Who are they? "She's dead because we made out," I thought. That was a natural thought, too. Betty and I were Baptists.

I could not remember going back to the locker room after Mom left. I could not remember the drive back home to our small house on Patton Street. The next time I was aware of where I was or what I was doing I was at home smashing the records that Betty and I often played when she came over. *Take Five. Hello Muddah, Hello Faddah. Ray Charles Sings Country."* Gogi Grant's *The Wayward Wind.* That was her song.

> *The wayward wind was a restless wind, a restless wind that yearns to wander; Oh, I was born the next of kin, the next of kin to a wayward wind.*

No more. She's dead. Who did it? How? Why? The last question I would never completely answer.

13

Shelly's Second Favorite Sport at Odessa Permian

CHAPTER III
The Rack

Daddy set off for work at the car wash every morning by at least 7:00 AM. It didn't matter what he'd done the night before, drinking 'til 3:00, playing poker at the American Legion, or visiting his main girlfriend, Dallas (I swear that was her name). He was always there, at the Rack.

I admired his fortitude as much as I resented his desire to "teach me the value of a dollar" by making me go to work with him every Saturday. Still, he believed that eight years old was a good time to learn life's hard lessons, so I went.

Looking back, I realize that I didn't really have to work too hard. Once the cars came out the end of the rack, right after they had passed through the blowers and got an initial rubdown, someone would drive them off the rack, make a sharp U turn, and pull them out front to the gas pumps for a final rubdown. My job, once they got out front, was to polish off the hubcaps.

Daddy had bought the car wash just the year before, in 1952. He had been driving through Odessa on his way back to California from picking up a couple of new cars from Detroit. He had driven all the way through Odessa and was having a beer and a burger at the "Nip and Sip" on Second Street when he figured that he should go back into town and clean off those cars before getting back to Fresno.

As luck would have it, the Odessa rack was nearly identical to the one he worked for in Fresno. It even had Chem Therm equipment. The place didn't have much business and it was obviously badly managed - nobody smiled at him when he drove in and his door panels were never touched - but Daddy thought it was a nice rack anyway.

When he got back home, he called back to the place and discovered that it was for sale for $12,000. That was an impossibly high price, but the Scotts who owned it (along with the three movie theaters in town) agreed to loan Daddy the full amount for 2 % interest.

So, we packed up Suziebell, our 1947 Plymouth, drove across the Rockies, and moved to Texas. I still remember walking down the "Strip" in Las Vegas on our way, but what impressed me even more were the lights of Odessa shining through the desert night as we drove into town somewhere near midnight on November 13, 1952.

We damned near starved in Odessa the first two years. Even though the town was growing, the car wash had been run into the ground and nothing Daddy did seemed to attract customers. The rack had costs whether or not we had customers--the mortgage payment, the electricity, and most of all the help. In the early '50s, car washes were labor intensive and most of the labor was black. Daddy paid everyone $1.00 an hour, which was standard, but he didn't hire and fire quite as ruthlessly as some racks did. That was because of the "Boys." The "Boys" had followed Daddy from Oberlin, LA to Fresno, CA to Odessa, TX. They were all male, all black, and all Cajun. Why they liked to work for Daddy, I'll never know for sure, but they were loyal to him and he was, more or less, loyal to them. Reflecting their Louisiana roots, they called Daddy, King Fish, my mom, Mama Fish, while I was, of course, Baby Fish. In a real sense the King Fish was taking care of our family plus five rambunctious, young, and hard working black families as well.

One day, Daddy got an idea. I would not be going to the car wash to work that Saturday. Instead I should ask Joe Bob Chapman and Dale Everrett, neighborhood kids, if they'd like to make a little spending money passing out leaflets that weekend. They said yes, so we were off and running. Daddy found a printer in town to produce a thousand single page leaflets of various colors-red, orange, yellow, and green. On each of these was printed the following message along with the address of Bill's Car Wash:

> ### STARTING NEXT SATURDAY
> ### 59-Cent Car Wash!
> ### with 18 or more gal. of gas
> ### $1.25 15-18 gal.
> ### $1.50 10-15 gal.
> ### $1.75 all others

It was a crude leaflet and a simple message. The three of us walked all over town passing them out. We hit houses, parking lots, and even pedestrians. The following Saturday morning Daddy decided to leave for the rack even earlier than usual. We pulled up into the lot at 6:45 AM. Even Daddy didn't know how to explain what we saw. Cars were lined up both ways around the block waiting for the 8:00 AM opening. I did not wipe down bumpers that day. Instead I stood at the juncture of the lines feeding into the entrance and helped sort out who was next in line to have his car vacuumed. I have often thought back to that morning as the beginning of my diplomatic career. It was also the beginning of my family's move up to the lower middle class. From that day on, business boomed and the Williams family could leave behind duplexes on unpaved roads and baloney sandwiches for dinner.

Daddy was asked to become the President of the Car Wash Association of America. Discounting car washes for the amount of gas sold became a national practice. He was proud of the honor, and he put the CWA certificate with his name on it up on the office wall, but he declined to attend the Association's meetings. He hated meetings and he would go nowhere that might expect him to wear a suit. He did, however, get on the phone to Southern Illinois to tell his brother Joe to come to Texas. What he said was blunt. "Joe, you won't have your precious god-damned carpenter's union down here, but at least, by god, you'll find work." Joe didn't like that sort of language and he sure didn't like the rough and tumble nature of an oil boomtown in the middle of the West Texas desert, but a man has to feed his family. Within weeks he packed up his wife and three girls and moved to Odessa. They moved in next door to us.

The Rack Before the Discount

CHAPTER IV
The Kid Preacher

Ferne Cliff Park in Goreville, Illinois is as pretty a place as a kid would ever want to see. It has statuesque trees, streams coming from the hills leading to a lake, and best of all caves. Families pour into it on Sunday afternoons for picnics and gatherings of all sorts. On many Sundays in the early 1930's, before Ferne Cliff became a State Park and right in the middle of the Depression, the Williams family and the Martin Family would drive down the dirt road that connected them to each other to the narrow, bumpy, rock-filled so-called road that led down to Ferne Cliff. The A.H. Martin Family was as close to society as possible in Goreville. A.H. owned the local Block plant, did a little farming, and helped bring a bank to town. The Williams family was a different lot.

Pete and Sarah (folks called her Sally) Williams were certainly respectable. Being poor in those days was not an embarrassment. Sally was beloved by all. She was kind and sweet and exceedingly gentle. Pete operated the little grocery store downtown, and many of the local high school kids worked there part time. The problem was that the whole family had lived upstairs in the back of the store for many, many years. The farmhouse had burned down when the oldest boy, Kink, was thirteen years old. Most folks in Goreville thought John, the eleven year-old, had actually set the fire. Well, some said, "set" the fire, and some said, "caused" the fire. Small town whispering could tell it both ways and not care which version was accurate, but inside the family the fire was easily explained. It was God's punishment for the wickedness and sin of the older boys. Smoking, drinking, cursing, even taking God's name in vain had done in the Williams family. They would forever feel the wrath.

Little John may or may not have caused the fire and he may or may not have done it intentionally, but he knew he was being punished for it nonetheless. Henceforth, he would follow the word of the Lord and behave. At least he would try. Many times after he would "backslide" with liquor or cigarettes, but he would seek solace in the Lord and he would always walk in the path of righteousness. He would even talk that way. Everyday he seemed to try to be more like his father. His Dad, Pete, after all had been the "Kid Preacher of Southern Illinois." At fourteen he had evangelized the coal miners over close to Carbondale and Marion. He had stood at the gape of the mineshafts and shared the word of the Lord day-in and day-out for over a year. Finally the miners got tired of hearing it and asked Pete if he didn't just want to come to work with them. He did until felled by a horrible cracking cough so bad that he had to leave the mines and take up farming. He may have left the mines but he never abandoned his Faith and he was determined that every member of his family would follow him in that "old time religion."

Little John, Joe to his friends, took to the lessons hard, but Kink, the oldest boy, never bought into it. Oh, he feared his father and he adored his mother, so he mostly did what he was told. He certainly did his chores around the house and he even looked around town for odd jobs to do that would help the family, but he wanted no part of religion. People who knew Kink well never knew a time when he didn't smoke, drink, or keep two girls going at once. By eleven he was smoking a pack of Camels daily, and he started drinking before then. If his body was a temple, it was a monument to personal excess not to clean living. He always smiled when repeating that particular line about himself. Joe disapproved of Kink's behavior, but he had to admit that prettier girls seemed to want to be around Kink. And the guys in town thought it was terrific that the two oldest Williams boys were always good for a dice game--even if Kink had to threaten to tell their parents about some sin Joe had committed before the younger brother would give in. Joe never forgot that committing that first sin was what would lead to the next one.

Two little brothers, Chet and Little Pete, and precious Mary followed behind Kink and Joe, but the great Williams Family Battles had been fought out with Joe and Kink. Besides just a month or so after Mary was born, Sally died in her rocking chair. She fell asleep in the chair one hot summer day and her heart simply gave out. The family had only recently moved from the store to the tiny house down the road from the Martins. The Depression was on and business was bad. Pete seemed lost in a fog the next few years and Kink and Joe in many ways raised themselves after Sally died. They looked after the little kids the best they could, but mostly they just began to get on with their own lives. Pete remarried. Joe became an avid member of the local Baptist Church and there he met Mary Belle Henderson. She was the closest thing to Sally Williams as anyone had ever seen. She was sweet, optimistic, and totally devoted to Jesus. Kink also thought she was an angel. After many long years of dating, Joe and Mary Belle got married just before World War II was over.

Kink himself married at age twenty in 1935. Absolutely everyone in Goreville, and especially everyone in the Williams' household, was astonished when he did. Not only was he not "the marrying kind," he married the local town catch, A.H. Martin's oldest daughter, Marian. She was the head cheerleader, the prettiest girl in school, and also a Baptist. She was also seeing Kink secretly and having a fine time at the parties they went to. Besides, she thought, she could straighten him out after they were married. The weekend they got married, he went to a barn dance alone, got drunk and had sex with another girl. That was Kink. Joe and Mary Belle started a family in 1943 with the birth of a daughter, Elizabeth Jean Williams. Marian convinced Kink after nine tumultuous years of marriage that a baby might bring them together as a family, so they had a child in 1944. That child was Shelton Lee Williams. Marian called him Shelly. Kink hated that name and rarely used it.

After the Second World War, Joe settled down just outside of Goreville. He was a carpenter, and there was plenty of work. He and Mary Belle built a three-bedroom house just outside of town. Two more children followed quickly and life looked pretty good. Kink and Marian had it a little rougher. Not that there weren't opportunities. Kink bought into a truck stop at West Vienna, IL. He managed it and Marian waited tables and kept the books. Unbeknownst to Marian, Kink also kept slot machines in a room upstairs in the back. Since he was also screwing the local sheriff's wife, she always warned him when the cops were coming. He would clear the room and hide the machines. Later when he cheated on the sheriff's wife, she didn't call him and he was busted. Had he not been a World War II Vet, the sheriff would have booked him. Instead he merely told him to go elsewhere.

Elsewhere proved to be first Crutherville, MO, then Oberlin, LA, then Fresno, CA, and then Odessa, TX. The Mob made him leave Missouri because they were taking over gambling in that area and the jukebox business that covered for the slots had to be sold at cost. In Louisiana he went into the sawmill business, but he lost his only two logging trucks to the Parrish sheriff's brother-in-law in a poker game. California was next, but he could find little to do there but work for a car wash. At first he was a regular employee but soon he became the manager. When he did, he sent for the "Boys," a collection of five young Cajun black young men who had worked on his sawmill in Oberlin. They all nearly starved to death in Fresno. Kink took up odd jobs to make it and one of them was to deliver new cars from Detroit to Fresno for the owner of the car wash, a rich and impatient man who wanted the new line of cars weeks before they came to California's new car lots. On one such trip Kink saw a car wash he decided to buy. After years of a gypsy life, he and his family settled in Odessa.

Joe and Mary Belle never intended to leave Southern Illinois. Little Pete, Chet, and Mary never did. But Joe somehow could never consistently find the work he needed to. The area declined somewhat after the War as the coal industry died down, but Southern Illinois University and the federal prison in Marion always had building projects. Joe worked off and on but he sustained a back injury on a job in Goreville and he had to lay off on occasion after that. For some reason, that did not seem like the whole explanation for why he didn't get work. He did talk a lot on the job. He seemed always either to be preaching in a holier than thou way or he seemed to be bragging. His church was the best church in four counties and his three girls were the smartest kids Johnson County had ever seen. His brother Kink had a pink Cadillac in Texas and he was the President of the Car Wash Association of America. Did anyone recall when as a teenager, Joe had outrun Jim Thorpe in a hundred-yard dash? No one even recalled that Jim Thorpe had been anywhere close to Goreville High when Joe ran track there, and certainly no one believed the nonsense about Kink being the President of anything. It was unclear why Joe didn't find more work, but he didn't. When Kink called in 1954 and said to come to Odessa where oil flowed like water and where every place you looked a new building was going up, Joe decided to relocate. The first few years he would in fact live right next door to his brother. As he left town, he visited Ferne Cliff Park one more time.

Little Pete, Kink, Grandpa Pete, and Uncle Joe

CHAPTER V
Be Good, Kids

Betty and I hated Thanksgiving and Christmas dinners. It all seemed so artificial to us-- as if we were one big happy family. At one time, our families had lived next door to each other. That's when she and I really became close. But her little brother, Joe Wayne, had been born, and we never went to her house while we lived twenty-five feet from each other. It could have been the new baby or it could be that the two little houses we lived in on Muskingum St. simply could not accommodate the nine of us. In any event, we did not start alternating Christmas at one house and Thanksgiving at the other until we had both moved, us to a nicer part of town and them to a marginally worse part of town.

Betty moved off 27th street and just west of Andrews Highway. None of the streets were paved in her neighborhood on Henderson Street, and they stayed that way until the late 60s. The houses were old and well worn, though none of them could be over fifteen years old. Some kind of Wire Company was in the lot across the street from Betty's. I always noticed the paper and other trash that had blown up against the rusted pipe fence that encircled the long tin shed that housed the Wire Company. Two blocks over and three blocks down was Betty's church, Friendship Baptist. It was in a small building with a small chapel. The whole place seemed claustrophobic to me, but her family loved it. It was "real hard shell."

Our family lived on Patton Street, just a block or so east of East County Road. We had a two-bedroom house in a nice neighborhood, and Highland Methodist Church was just a block away. Best of all I was in the Permian High School district with all my friends I went to school with at Bonham Junior High. Betty's house was in the Odessa High School zone. Permian opened in 1959, and we knew from day one that we were going to be one of the greatest football programs in Texas history. How did we know that? I don't know, but damned if it didn't turn out to be true. I am convinced that where we lived and where we went to school affected how both Betty and I turned out, but it may well have been something more fundamental.

It could not have been genes because we were essentially from the same gene pool. Our fathers were completely different but exactly alike. My dad was a sinner and a scoundrel. Hers claimed to be a saint. I had been aware of my dad's fall from grace since I was eight years old. At age fourteen, he had arranged a trip to the Carlsbad Caverns with Betty's parents, another uncle, and me. He told my mom to stay home to look after our car wash. He then called his girlfriend, Dallas, to join us on the trip. They walked hand-in-hand behind me as I struggled to learn the mysteries of stalactites and stalagmites. On the way back to Odessa, the men and Dee were drinking whiskey from a bottle when a Highway patrol man pulled us over.

"Gee, Officer, I could not have been going eighty," my dad had said. "It must be a mis-calibration of the speedometer I just got repaired."

"Oh, sure," the cop said. "Do you have a receipt for this repair work?'

My dad leaned into his pink Cadillac, opened the glove compartment and pulled out a repair receipt from "Charley Sparks

26

Auto." On it was something like: "Received $40.00, speedometer repair." The patrolman was incredulous, but he told Daddy to have Charley to look at the speedometer again when we got back to Odessa. Never once did the cop suspect my dad had been drinking, but as soon as he got back in the car, Daddy was obviously impaired. He did mention that Charley Sparks was a good friend.

"You better take over, Shelly Bill," he said to his fourteen-year-old son with no license. I drove back to Odessa from just outside of El Paso with three drunken adults and my sober aunt Mary Belle, who found nothing to comment on or complain about the whole four hundred mile trip.

The next day, Daddy pulled me aside and told me "we don't want to upset your mother, so best not to mention Dee was on the trip." I knew I could not mention it to my mom, and I also knew that my years of trying to get them back together were fruitless. And now I was implicated in her betrayal. The thing was he always made me feel guilty for what was wrong with their marriage or with my mom herself.

"Exactly," Betty would say. "That is exactly what my dad does to me. If he can't find work or gets sick or one of the other kids gets sick, I must have done something wrong."

"I don't love him or the Lord enough or I wear too much make-up. I call boys or sneak out with them."

"I bring 'God's punishment down on our household,'" she quoted him. And like my Daddy, her dad would threaten to leave or threaten to punish or occasionally threaten to kill himself. All because we were bad kids.

OK, truth be known, I bought this message more than just a little bit. I tried to be good. I never drank, never smoked, never did anything adventurous with girls, never gambled, but I did have carnal thoughts--lots of carnal thoughts. I didn't buy it completely, but Reverend Richard Philpot at the Second Baptist Church told us that having carnal thoughts was a sin and all sins were equal to all other sins. Committing murder was no more or no less a sin than having a carnal thought, but if I believed in Jesus and if I asked forgiveness, all my sins could be wiped away. I believed Reverend Philpot, and I knew what he was trying to say, but even at the tender age of ten, I recall wondering if maybe Hitler's sins were a teeny more impressive, a teeny harder to forgive, than mine. Still I believed.

Betty did, too, but as we grew up, she had a different take on the whole carnal thoughts issue. If an act is no greater or lesser sin than a thought, why not commit the act? Then you could ask for forgiveness.

I admit that her argument held certain logic for me, but it just didn't square with being a good boy. Besides, my dad committed the acts and, even if he did ask God's forgiveness, which I doubted, I thought two other people in our family would be much better off if he had had only carnal thoughts. I made that argument and Betty agreed, but she also pointed that that she was not married and even though it was God's plan for girls to be mothers, she was going to put it off as long as possible.

At Christmas and Thanksgiving, Betty and I always bolted down our food and then went out to a car to sit and talk. We discussed our fathers, religion, movies, how much she hated football, and eventually sex. She started having sexual experiences long before I did. She was so bright and natural discussing sex, it almost seemed to be OK to do so. We would sit close on these occasions, and sometimes I would get hard. She would move her leg or my penis if it got uncomfortable for her, but she seemed fine with it. She showed me how to kiss and then how to French kiss. We didn't make out like boyfriend and girlfriend, but sometimes the practice went on a bit longer than it should. This went on for years, and even after she started screwing guys, it never went further than a few kisses. We were Kissing Cousins and sometimes she would tell girlfriends that I was her "Kissin' Cuz."

As we grew older, our personal fortunes steadily diverged. I went to Permian, played football, made good grades, and got elected to the Student Council. Betty had theater and little else. She loved reading about movie stars and she loved to be on the stage where she could be anyone but herself. She seemed less sure of herself as she went into the latter part of her junior year of High School, though she managed to get Juliet in Romeo and Juliet balcony scene. Most of the time she hated school, hated her dad, and hated Odessa, By God, Texas.

Occasionally we would talk on the phone. I would be studying in my bedroom/den (my mom had moved from the master bedroom to my old room) and Betty would call just to say hi. One night the phone rang and she didn't say "hi," she said: "Guess who I fucked tonight?" It was the first time I ever heard a girl say fuck. The boy was Will Rosebud, a high profile athlete, class officer, and all around great guy. Even though he went to OHS, I knew him well, and I knew his girlfriend, a cheerleader. I admit I was shocked, but Betty made the whole thing sound so funny. How horny he was; how he had to pretend not to know her at Tommy's; how she had to slow him down. "Jesus, it was like I was back to teaching you, Shell."

"Don't say, Jesus," I chastised her. "What happened next?"

"We did it in about two minutes. Two minutes isn't long enough, Shell. Remember that when it comes time."

I did.

Suddenly she said: "Don't worry, Shell, I never tell anyone I am your cousin. Never"

"Betty, who don't you tell? I'll call them up right now. I am not ashamed of you, Betty Jean Williams."

"Well, you should be," she said.

That was the last time she ever called. At the time I thought about her call. I really was not ashamed of her. She was mixed up, but she didn't want to hurt anybody. She had real talent. She was just not meant for Odessa, Texas. That's all. And I really could not believe whom she had fucked that night.

CHAPTER VI
You Been Hittin' That?

"Bill's Car Wash" on Dixie Street was an Odessa institution. The owner, Kink Williams, changed his name to Bill Williams because no one knew the name Kink, the nick name the kids in Goreville, IL gave him because of his black, "kinky" hair. No one called him by his real name either, Marshall Henry Williams.

The "Boys" at the car wash called him King Fish or boss man. He called them "niggers" when they weren't around, but there were good niggers and bad niggers in his opinion. Good ones worked hard and didn't complain. Bad ones didn't show up for work or took huge advances on their weekly pay.

For me, Baby Fish, the Boys were a different story. From the time I was six, I knew "the Boys" as my friends. One in particular, a sixteen-year old named Grover Romulus Cezar III, was a constant in my life for sixteen years. Everyone called him Gro. Even as a teen Gro treated me like a real person, not the boss' son, not a little white boy, not as a baby, as a real person. Consequently, I loved and adored Gro, and I never used the word nigger. Never.

Gro, his brother James, and three other guys came to Odessa to work at the car wash in 1953. By the mid '50s, only the Cezar brothers were left, and Gro had become in fact, but not in name, the manager of the car wash. Once, on a busy Saturday afternoon, a man from Mississippi brought his beat up old junk heap into the rack to get it washed. My dad, the owner, was not there. He was across from car wash sipping beers at "The Joker," a beer joint that somehow happened to be on the edge of the car wash lot. The owner of this impossibly small place--only five seats at the bar--was Dallas Lanier. Her trailer sat next to "The Joker." King Fish usually started drinking there by around 10:00 AM, sometimes closer to noon.

When the man from Mississippi discovered that the owner was not there to take his buck seventy-five, he started looking for a white person to whom he could give the money. Only Gro and I were there. "I a'int giving no money to no nigger" is what he told Gro. Gro pointed him to me and told the man to give the money to me. The good citizen from Mississippi was somewhat confused because the black man seemed to be pointing to a child. He stormed toward me and shouted: "I a'int giving no money to no nigger. Where's the boss at?"

"He's not here, Sir," I said. "You can give it to him," pointing at Gro.

"I a'int giving no money to no nigger," he repeated helpfully. "Here, you take it."

Now I was allowed to take the money. In fact I took money all the time. I even sometimes helped Daddy hand out advances on the weekly pay, and I sometimes helped Mom balance the books at the end of the day. I knew my way around the cash register no matter how young I was. Nevertheless, I looked at the gentleman from the great state of Mississippi, threw up my hands, and said clearly and logically:

"Sir, I am only ten years old. I can't take money. Mr. Cezar is the only person here who can take your money."

I once again pointed to the young black man who was at that very moment ringing up another customer. The confused son of the South did not know what to do except to reiterate his message that had apparently not sunk in to these thick-sculled Texans. "I a'int giving no money to no nigger!" With that last declaration, he threw his dollar bill and three quarters on the asphalt surface of the car cash lot. He got into his battered old '50 Chevy and he squealed out of the parking lot.

I thought the man's departure was funny, and I believed that I had personally struck a blow for justice and against racism. Gro thought otherwise. After we worked on clearing out the next several cars from the front of the car wash and before a couple of others had come off the rack, Gro grabbed me and marched me into the store room where the extra soap, chamois, and car chains were stored. Gro cuffed me on the back of the head and growled. "What do you think you're doin'?"

"But," Gro, I protested, "That man called you a nigger. He did it two or three times."

"Yes, he did, Shelly Bill (Gro called me what Daddy called me), but don't you pay no attention to the likes of him. I surely don't."

"But, Gro," I pleaded, "that's just not right."

"Bill, there's a lotta niggers in this world. Some are black and some are white. I a'int one of them. That man was. That's all I need to know and you too. Don't go messin' with that man's mind 'cause you can't teach him nothin' anyway."

There may have been important folk wisdom in what Gro told me, but actually I never quite accepted the point. From that day on, I almost always got into a fight when a white person used the term "nigger." The only times I didn't fight at the mention of that word was when either my father or one of my closest buddies used it-- and I hoped someday to be far away from all of them. I knew he couldn't teach them anything anyway.

Most of the guys, and one woman, at the car wash did not go out of their way to teach me "Life's Lessons." Well, they didn't intend to anyway. I learned a lot from them nevertheless. John Wesley "Fat Man" Jackson, T-Bone Johnson, Willie Gamble,

Freddie Mae Jackson (no relation to Fat Man), James Cezar, and little Leonard Jones were a weekly part of my life for ten years, from eight to eighteen. They took me to the "other side of the tracks" to have barbecue chicken and red soda pop; they took me to parties where folks danced "The Mashed Potato" and "The Twist" long before the white teenagers ever heard of those dances; and, as I got older, they talked to me endlessly about sex.

"King Fish been hittin' that," said Willie Gamble in reference to Kink Williams' personal relationship with Ms. Freddie Mae Jackson, a sexy but not very pretty lady of thirty who worked at the car wash.

"Thanks, Willie, I really needed to know that," I said.

"I'ma just tellin' ya so you don't go hittin' it yourself and making your Daddy mad," Willie replied. "You gettin' grow'd, you know." I was fifteen.

"OK, Willie, good advice. I'll watch out." We both laughed because we knew that I would never try to have sex with Freddie Mae and both knew that Freddie Mae would never have sex with me.

One day in 1960 Betty Jean Williams brought her car in for a wash. She drove a clunky 1955 Oldsmobile. Instead of pulling her car into the vacuum area, she stopped fifteen-twenty yards from it and simply got out of her car. Black jeans hugged her skinny frame. She also had on a black T-shirt and black loafers. Her long blonde hair was pulled back. Had her beatnik appearance not made her stand out, her demeanor would have. Stepping out of the car seemed to render her instantly helpless. She looked this way and that, and she wrung her hands. The Boys had no idea what to make of her, but I reacted quickly. I put her back into the passenger's side of the car, and then drove the vehicle into the vacuum. I did both sides of the car with the vacuum and then jumped in the car as the chain pulled it slowly up to the rack.

Fat Man and T-Bone soaped and steam-cleaned the tires; Willie and James lathered it with soap after it passed through the water spray; Leonard and Freddie Mae wiped it down with chamois after it passed thorough another water spray and came through the powerful blowers. No one got inside to do the windows because the girl and I were in there talking. When the car reached the end of the rack, I did not make a left U-turn and drive it to the front. Instead I made a right U-turn and parked it along the side of the building next to the office. We talked some more. Eventually I got out of the car and walked back to the front. The girl drove away.

I went back to work as if nothing at all at happened. Eventually Fat Man and Freddie Mae walked over to me and stood silently for a bit. All the cars cleared out and they spoke their minds.

"Say, Fish," Freddie Mae said.

"Yeah," I replied.

"Me and the Fat Man been wondering. You know, about the girl that was just here."

"Yeah," I said cautiously.

"You been hittin' that?"

CHAPTER VII

Boom Town

Odessa, Texas in the 1950s was the ultimate oil boomtown. Its population exploded from slightly over 30,000 in 1950 to over 100,000 in 1960. These folks came from other parts of Texas and around the nation, but all Odessans, new and old, were knee deep in the oil business either directly or indirectly and they were almost all some kind of rock-ribbed, free-market conservative. Their politics generally ran to the extreme right. Theodore H. White in The New Republic in 1954 said that if McCarthyism was the "nation's disease, Odessa was its hospital ward." Religion was usually the old time variety as practiced on Sunday, but in truth the good folks of Odessa worshipped the Friday Night Lights of Texas High School football. The passion, the intensity, and the importance of high school football often brought as many as 15,000 people out on a Friday night to Barrett stadium. On alternating Friday nights beginning in 1959, they watched either the red-and-white clad Bronchos or the new Permian Panthers who wore black uniforms with white helmets. In Odessa Oil was God, but high school football was King. Odessa was never a tranquil town, but folks there had a pretty clear worldview.

Politics did not much interest Odessans except to denounce politicians. The blamed fools did not understand the need for an oil depletion allowance or the dangers of reliance on foreign oil. They talked about crazy stuff like integration, welfare spending, being soft on the Communists, and more taxes. Odessans were opposed to it all. All Odessans were opposed to it all. The John Birch Society held its annual state conventions in Odessa, and everyone voted Republican. In 1964 when Lyndon Johnson won a landslide across America, Barry Goldwater carried every election box in Ector County. No doubt some of the remaining found Goldwater just a bit too soft. The Odessa American even ran an editorial in 1961 against public education in principle. Folks just needed to teach their kids at home and not trust them to the socialists and government bureaucrats who ran public schools.

To the kids in Odessa public schools none of this talk affected them one bit. They accepted the political views of their parents, wasted no time in learning about events of the day, and focused on Friday night football. The public high schools in Odessa in 1961 reflected the oil boom that built Odessa and the baby boom that hit the United States. The black kids in town went to Blackshear High, which existed from 1948 until 1965 when it was merged with Ector High School, a school that came into existence in 1957. Both of these schools were smaller than the other two high schools in town, Odessa High School and the gleaming new Permian High School built in 1959 on the east side of town. Each of them had nearly 1200 students. The kids at Blackshear and Ector were mostly poorer black, Hispanic, or less numerous poor white kids. At OHS the kids were mostly white with a few Hispanics. Permian was almost monolithically white but a few Hispanics were here and there.

On the streets of Odessa at night, kids from Blackshear were largely invisible. They stayed south of the tracks. Ector kids showed up downtown sometimes but not in great numbers. They tended to like Roy's drive-in on Eighth Street, whereas the OHS and Permian kids overwhelmed Tommy's Drive-In on Andrews Highway. Tommy Lombardo had built the place in the summer of 1958, and it became the immediate hangout for hundreds of OHS and Permian kids. Hot cars and clunky cars jammed its lot at noon and after school.

"Cruising Tommy's" was not only the best thing to do on Saturday night; it seemed like the only thing to do. Boys met girls there and boys hung out there on their own. Unlike Roy's or Day's Drive-in down town, fights almost never broke out there. Tommy would ban any boy for fighting for any reason there. The "no fighting" rule and the cherry cokes guaranteed a mixture of boys and girls and a huge turn out. Forty years later adults would look back at the night that the OHS and Permian cheerleaders alternated conducting cheers on the walk way of the huge billboard overlooking Tommy's as one of the most magical nights in their entire lives.

Pep rallies and drive-ins were wonderful but football games were life itself. In 1959, the year Permian was built, OHS was 7-3 and Permian was 3-7. OHS lost to the great Abilene dynasty of Coach Chuck Moser by a mere 7-0. It beat the new upstart Permian by a "not as close as it looks" 14-6. OHS in truth dominated that game. The remarkable thing about the game on the field was the lack of personal hostility the players on each side had for one another. Odessa coaches—the assistant coaches anyway—at both schools had a habit of demonizing the upcoming opponents.Abilene teams were rich, satisfied, and smug. Winning the 4-A state championship four years in a row probably had that effect on them. Big Spring kids were "white trash." Midland kids were just rich softies. Out of district teams often magically transformed into godless communists or worse. Dallas kids and Dallas schools were beyond the pale—big city, rich, liberal, worthless. But the kids at OHS and Permian were really the same people. They had gone to the same junior high schools, belonged to the same social clubs, or High Ys (boys) and Tri Hi Ys (girls), same scouting troops, and more importantly had played football, basketball, and baseball in various youth leagues for a decade.

On the field during the game, the OHS and Permian kids played hard in the fall of 1959, but everyone knew the outcome. OHS had the studs and Permian had played a few good games, but it was no match for the Bronchos. An end, Johnny Hodges, for the

Bronchos often broke up players on both teams with wisecracks at the line of scrimmage. "Damned coaches should know better than to think this fucking play will work." "Sure hope we get beer at half time." Calling to the Permian lineman, Roger Rankin, "Hey, Corvette, your girlfriend was great in bed last night." No one on that field would ever dream that Permian would come to dominate the series after only a few years, and no one would ever dream that in two years it would be easy for each side's assistant coaches to motivate their boys across a bitter cross town rival.

Neither Mack Herring nor I was viewed an elite athlete in Odessa. Mack was skinny, not very graceful, and not terribly fast. As a sophomore he was buried on the junior varsity second team and he never started when he moved to varsity his junior year. He played because West Texas boys played football if they had any size at all. His dad wanted him to. Mack preferred to hunt and fish. He liked being alone, but football gave him some status. He did like some of the guys on the team. There were no "Mack Herring" football stories around town. No famous hits. No miracle fumble recoveries. No spectacular touchdown receptions. He was on the team.

I was equally unknown to the newspapers and to the general public. On the Permian team, however, I had a reputation. Curiously for a guy who always made jokes and avoided fights, I was a tremendous scrapper when I put on a football uniform. At 5'6" and 165 pounds I was improbably small to play 4-A football, but then Permian tended to have small, fast players anyway. I had started on defense as a junior varsity player played behind Roger Rankin at middle guard my junior year. Rankin hurt his shoulder toward the end of the season and I acquitted myself fairly well as the starter. That second year of Permian's existence the Panthers dethroned Abilene High 19-13 and we beat OHS 27-14. We went 8-2 during the regular season, won the district championship, and then, shockingly lost to El Paso Ysleta in the state playoffs. The OHS game was spirited but this time Permian had the studs.

The talk around Odessa after the fall of 1960 got somewhat

heated about the coaches at Permian and at OHS. The OHS coach, Lacy Turner, was too nice a guy and not a winner. The Permian coach, Ted Dawson, had backed his way into the district championship. Had OHS not beaten Midland High, Permian would not have won district. In some towns 8-2 would be a good record. In Odessa in the early '60s not only was 8-2 not good enough, but after a 9-1 record in the fall of 1961, Ted Dawson, Tubby Ted his players called him, was fired. The San Angelo Bobcats' coach, Emory Bellard, out coached him in a 15-0 victory and thus "stole" Permian's district championship. The victory bell, an actual bell, set on two wheels and pulled by enthusiastic team supporters, would change hands. Dawson had to go. Players in both programs were aware of these criticisms, and some even joined in. None of them truly comprehended the absurd lengths that adults in Odessa would go to win high school football games or ruin the careers of coaches who had performed at an excellent level for years on end.

At both schools football was king, but both also had outstanding bands, debate teams, Student Councils, and much more. At OHS the sense of social hierarchy was even greater than at Permian, but football status, while of great import, did not rule all. Wealth, family status, and certainly looks were critical. There was a hint of greater formality in the classroom, and there was the inevitable fact that OHS was a much older institution with longer held traditions than the newly built Permian. At Permian, it seemed like talent, looks and quick wit determined "popularity." The groups of kids who hung out together were usually all white, yes, but many of them never knew what their friends' parents did for a living. They visited each others' homes regardless of whether some were four and five bedroom brick ranch houses and some were tiny, two bedroom, wood-framed duplexes. At Permian, at that time, these differences seemed simply not to matter to the students. Personality and talent ruled at Permian, though playing football certainly helped.

The reactions of the two schools to Betty Williams' death in March, 1961, was almost immediate. Most OHS kids were shocked that a popular boy had been accused of killing a marginal, unimportant oddball like Betty. She had a "reputation." She put out easily, and while some knew that Mack dated her, they also knew that he never took her out in public. She never wore his football jacket; never went to the Scott Theater with him on Saturday night; and never met his parents. In fact they went together and broke up repeatedly. Betty would stay mostly true to Mack when they were together, but she had other "friends" when they broke up. Betty's senior year, Mack's junior year, had been tumultuous for her. She had played lead role in several drama productions the year before but the new drama teacher did not select her for any lead roles and in the spring production she had gotten no role at all in Winterset. Curiously and ironically Mack had tried out for the play and had gotten a lead role, playing Trock, a young man who commits a murder and suffers no remorse. Mack's "problem" of being accused of killing Betty sparked concerned phone calls to him, visits from friends, and no seeming diminution of his popularity.

At Permian Mack was a murderer. It did not matter that the police investigation revealed that Betty had asked him to kill her. It did not matter that Betty was on OHS' societal margins. Mack had no right to kill her. He could have gone to her parents, the police, or a counselor, if she asked him to do it. He did not have to pull the trigger. He had no right to play God or allow her to use him as a vehicle of her suicide. To some, Betty was my cousin, and I was popular at Permian. They chose Betty. How could those snooty OHS kids react so blindly to the death of a fellow teen? There were some kids at both schools who adopted the majority opinion of the other school, but for the most part OHS and Permian spilt down the middle. Odessa itself split down the middle, East against Mack and West for him-- East for Betty, and West against her. Cross-town friends who tried to have conversations about the event often ended up at odds. The OHS-Permian game the following year would have none of the easy camaraderie of the first two games in the series. It never did again.

West Texas Worship

--Dan Setterberg

CHAPTER VIII
"Washed in the Blood"

Friendship Baptist Church was overflowing. People were standing in back and on the sides of the chapel room. Every pew except the front two rows was full. The front pews were reserved for the family. All morning my parents and Betty's parents had been huddled in the tiny kitchen in the tiny house on Henderson Street. I remember very little about the morning, except it was the day I started drinking coffee. None of us talked about Betty, the killing, or what the church was going to be like. We were simply going through the motions, letting the day's events unfold. Neither my uncle nor my father seemed particularly edgy or upset that morning. My aunt and my mother busied themselves in the kitchen. The other kids in Betty's family stayed in the den playing and arguing as usual. When we left for the church, we had no idea what were walking into or how much emotion would sweep us away.

My only reference points for the setting that day are two courtroom scenes from two black and white movies, *Inherit the Wind* and *To Kill A Mockingbird*. A huge, silent crowd of men and women dressed in plain black suits and plain black dresses awaited us. Most looked like they had never worn such garb for any other occasion except this one. The men had badly cut hair, and the women for the most part had their hair pulled straight back. It suddenly occurred to me that my mother was the only woman in the room who had her hair "done" for the occasion. The whole crowd, kids included, watched us every step of the way from the back of the chapel down to the front rows. I just wanted them to look the other way and let us proceed in peace. I was holding my mother's elbow as we walked. My aunt was holding my uncle's arm as if to keep him upright. It was a short distance but the longest walk I ever made.

The coffin was closed. I had never been to a funeral in my life, so I had not thought of the body and the coffin. But how could the coffin be opened? Not after the way she died. Uncle Joe started to cry, no, to wail, the second he saw the coffin. He sobbed uncontrollably throughout the service. He moaned during the two hymns the congregation sang and his emotions made the second hymn all the more powerful and moving. It was her favorite hymn.

Never Alone.

"I've seen the light - ning flash - ing.
And heard the thun - der roll,
I've felt sin's break - ers dash - ing.
Try - ing to con - quer my soul
I've heard the voice of Je - sus.
Tell - ing me to fight on,
He pro - mised never to leave me.
Nev - er to leave me a -lone.
No, nev - er a - lone...No, nev - er alone.
He promised nev - er to leave me.
Nev - er to leave me alone.

The irony of this beautiful song overwhelmed me. I was alone in a crowded room. Betty was alone in the coffin. Whatever comfort the song provided to others in the room, its impact on me was the opposite. I felt alone.

The preacher was a short, stout man with greying hair. I thought he looked like an insurance salesman. His message related to the first hymn we sang and then to the scripture. The hymn was --

"Washed in the Blood."

Have you been to Jesus for the cleansing power?
Are you washed in the blood of the Lamb?
Are you fully trusting in His grace this hour?
Are you washed in the blood of the Lamb?

The scripture was from the King James version of the Bible, Revelations 1:5.

And from Jesus Christ, who is the faithful witness, and the first begotten of the dead, and the prince of the kings of the earth. Unto him that loved us, and washed us from our sins in his own blood.

Betty's tragic death should not dismay us. Her sins have been washed away. She had put her faith in Jesus, accepted him into her heart, believed in him and in everlasting life.

True, I had never been to a funeral before. But what was supposed to be happening? Why didn't the preacher talk about Betty, her sense of humor, her devotion to the church, her love for little children? This was just another sermon. Yes, Betty had been "saved," but who was going to explain the mystery of her death. Why did she die? How could God allow this?

Uncle Joe interrupted my thoughts. His wailing and sobbing got out of control. I began to listen to him instead of the preacher.

"No, Betty Jean." "No sister." "Don't leave me, Girl." Damn, I thought. This is too much. It's not your funeral. Stop!

But he didn't stop. He cried more loudly and he wrenched his body around as if he were struggling to get up. Mary Belle held him back.

47

"No, Joe, No. Sit back, Daddy."

My dad slid forward in his pew watching his brother's every move. My mother cried softly to herself. I was stricken with the thought that Joe was going to fall on the floor or talk in tongues or faint. Suddenly he pulled free of Mary Belle and started toward the coffin itself. Before Joe's movements could even register with me, Daddy jumped over the front pew and pulled his anguished brother back to his seat.

"No, Kink, I have to say good-bye. My baby's dead. My baby's gone." As he sobbed, Daddy held him and looked straight ahead. The preacher had stopped in mid-sentence. The crowd looked on in horror. No one knew what to do next. My dad looked up at the insurance man preaching the gospel and gave him a direct command: "Go on."

The preacher finished his sermon, but I am certain that no one heard a word. I didn't. In fact, the remainder of the service, the ride to the gravesite, and the brief service there are a blurry memory. As we got back into the family car, Daddy simply fell into the driver's seat. He was exhausted and he was crying. In my sixteen years, I had never seen him in a church and I had never seen him cry. I was not in tears. I wanted answers. Why did she die? Why did he kill her? Was it my fault?

As we returned to Odessa, my family's car pulled away from the procession as we passed Permian High School. My baseball team had a game. I had decided to play because I did not want to go back to my uncle's house. I had to get away from him. Only my mother supported my decision--she always did--but it did not matter. I resolved from that day forward that nothing my parents said to me would ever affect my decisions again. Betty and I were on our own now.

The coach and the team were stunned to see me dressed out when I entered the dugout. They applauded. I did not expect to play, but Coach Cook inserted me in the fifth inning. I got two hits in that game and went two for four in the second game of the double header. Fortunately no one ever hit a ball at me in right field. We won both games handily, though I never knew exactly whom we were playing. I thought it odd that in the locker room after the game that no one noticed that I was a completely different person.

Our Betty

-- Dan Setterberg

CHAPTER IX
Star of Stage and Screen

The first time I ever realized that Betty had become a woman we were inside Tommy's dining room but not together. I was in the far corner of the room watching two OHS guys play chess, a game I have never mastered, and Betty had her back turned to everyone in the place. She had both hands on the jukebox; her knees were slightly bent and she was moving to the beat of *Little Bitty Pretty One*. Her head and her butt kept time to the music while her feet remained virtually stationary. Her blue jeans were tight; her white T-shirt did not conceal the fact that she wore no bra; and she was wearing no shoes. Eventually every boy in the room began staring at her. Several girls with either pony tails or Doris Day bubble cuts walked in, glanced disgustedly at her, and quickly diverted their eyes. Betty was breaking any number of rules that hot summer afternoon, the most egregious of which was the unspoken law of Tommy's: "No Girls Stay Inside of Tommy's Dining Room."

"Hey Betty," I said, approaching her after the song ended. "What are you up to?"

"Hey, Shell, how are you, Cuz? You been here long?"

"A bit. Just watching smart people play chess," I responded, and then motioning to the door, "Wanna go for a ride?"

"Let's do it!" Betty gushed. We didn't do this often with my sports and work schedule, but I loved it when we got to take off together. Next to cruising Tommy's, "driving around" was the second most common teenage activity in Odessa. Dividing the town east and west were the major arteries of 2nd St., 8th St., 27th St, and eventually 42nd St. (on which Permian would be built). The lower the number the older the section of town. The major arteries north and south were West County Rd. and East County Rd., but in between them was Andrews Highway, which turned into Grant St. downtown. Years later some of these streets would change names, but in the late '50s and early '60s these were our highways and byways of life. As much as we loved to encircle Tommy's, we also ceaselessly circled Odessa itself. Gas was cheap and privacy was priceless, so we drove. Betty and I headed out of Tommy's by turning right on Andrews Highway, drove down to 8th St., turned east up to East County Rd., hooked a left north there to 27th St., took another left back west, and ended up back at Tommy's. We didn't stop. Instead we repeated the same path without comment and without even considering another route. The whole journey took an hour-and-a-half and I completed perhaps three sentences the whole time.

"Life is beautiful, Shell. Someday we're gonna get out of this town. I am definitely going to be an actress. Can't you see me on the Jack Parr Show?" She didn't even wait for a response. "Oh, did you see Jonathan Winters on there last night? He did his little green men from Mars routine. He's crazy, too, you know?"

She knew I had seen it, and she knew I loved Winters. Almost everyone in town in those days was a TV junkie. Most kids and their parents preferred Gunsmoke, What's My Line? or The 64 Thousand Dollar Question, but few stayed up to watch Jack Parr. At least few admitted doing so. Jack Parr was too emotional for most West Texas men and, in truth, he was simply too effeminate for anyone from West Texas to admit liking. Betty and I were Jack Parr fans. We often discussed guests and she would frequently mimic them. She did a wicked Za Za Gabor, a hilarious Ma Frickett, and a rather touching Jack Parr himself. Our second favorite show was on Saturday nights, the Garry Moore Show. It featured our favorite new comedian, Carol Burnett, whom Betty could "do" perfectly. While most kids talked about girlfriends, proms, football, and hunting, Betty and I talked about actors, their talents, and what lay ahead for her.

"You know, it's not a bad thing that we're from Odessa, Shell. Carol Burnett's from San Antonio and Debbie Reynolds is from some small town somewhere. Not everyone is from New York City like Elaine May or Anne Meara." Betty and I assumed we were the only people in all West Texas, much less Odessa, who knew of Elaine May, Mike Nickols, or the shocking Lenny Bruce.

"I don't like Lenny Bruce" I told her "He's sacrilegious and he uses horrible language."

"Don't pay attention to what he says, Shell. Listen to why he says it," she said.

"Like using words like nigger, wop, kike and stuff like that," I retorted, my emerging liberalism duly engaged. "And saying things like Eleanor Roosevelt slept with Chiang Kai Shek? I don't even know what a kike is," I said.

"It's a bad word for a Jewish person, Shell, and Lenny is using those words publicly because he knows people use them privately while hiding their true feelings. Lenny Bruce is a truth teller. He says it out loud. He says that America is 'in bed' with a brutal dictator while it claims to be defending freedom. This whole country says one thing and does another. Lenny is making us face reality."

That is what I loved about Betty. She had ideas, and she expressed them. When she wanted to, she could be totally, brutally honest, even about herself. She saw acting as a way to tell emotional truths. As naïve as I was, I saw politics as a way to do that. I was already thinking about public office, the Foreign Service, or, more likely, teaching political science as a vehicle for "making the world better."

"No, Shell, too many compromises. Art, theater, and literature are the best way to tell the truth. You should read *On the Road* by Jack Kerhouac, you'd see! We have to burn like a flame, Shell! There are too many secrets in the country, too many injustices. You can't just tell people that racism, war, and poverty are wrong You have to make them feel it. Drama, especially comedy, are the best weapons we've got. I know it's true."

As we drove, I waived at a dozen or more kids. I even once, while stopped at a red light on Grant St., rolled down the window and exchanged pleasantries with an old friend, Jean Smith from OHS. Betty never stopped talking and she never got annoyed that I was only half listening to her dissertation on the art and politics of our time. While she was not manic, she was also not to be deterred. She was bursting with ideas and she had all the energy of newly converted missionary. I loved that I was one of the persons she assumed to be part of her faith. For the most part it was true, but my inspiration was John Kennedy, not Lenny Bruce.

What I loved about my cousin though was that she could be both analytical and so full of life simultaneously. In my vast experience with women by the age of sixteen, thoughtful girls were not especially fun and fun girls were decidedly not thoughtful. Betty set a higher standard for me. More than one West Texas kewpie doll fell in my estimation after responding, "Who's that?" after I mentioned Nichols and May or Dean Rusk. Maybe they should not have known a cutting edge comedy team or a virtually invisible Secretary of State, but I expected them to anyway. I couldn't help it.

What I didn't know when Betty and I finished our marathon tour of the main streets of Odessa was that for all her "truth telling" rhetoric, Betty was in fact "Queen of Secrets." As I let her out at her house, I never would have guess that Betty's sole appearance on TV would not be on the Jack Parr Show. Instead it would be in a small black and white photograph cut from her senior yearbook on the evening news over a caption: "Local Girl Dies Tragically." From that sole TV appearance to this day, the funny, smart, enthusiastic Betty I knew became the morose, troubled, strange girl who asked Mack Herring to kill her.

Talk about an injustice.

Betty's Junior Picture

CHAPTER X
The Play's the Thing

"That woman is horrible." Betty had only a very few close personal friends, but Annabelle Jackson was one of them. Miss Woodward, the new drama teacher, was the object of Betty's wrath and frustration. She had swooped into Odessa like a Queen Bee. She may have been Tallulah Bankhead wherever she went to college, but to Betty and Annabelle, she was evil incarnate. What she didn't know as a teacher was that kids don't care where a teacher went to college, Texas Tech in this case, or what she has written, performed or accomplished. They care how she treats them and how well or badly she makes them feel. As a young teacher, Miss Woodward had not yet learned that, and she made Betty feel like a nobody. Betty had definitely been a somebody her junior year. She had been in Peck's *Bad Boy*, *Puss and Boots* and, most importantly, Juliet in the balcony scene of *Romeo and Juliet*. An English teacher before, Miss Hollaway, seemed to like Betty and even told her that she had "potential." When Betty said the word "potential," she mimicked Mrs. Hollaway's overemphasis on the first syllable.

Miss Woodward saw no such potential in Betty. She saw very little to like and in a way she seemed like she was trying to compete with Betty for claim to be the most visible theater person at OHS. It was no contest. Betty's ego was pint-sized compared to Miss Woodward's. Miss Woodward could reduce Betty to tears by simple acts of discourtesy. Betty would answer a question in class and Miss Woodward would fix a stare at her and then turn to another student. She would write glowing praise on one student's paper and mark a B+. She would give Betty an A- without so much as mark on the paper, as if she had not read it at all, just slapped a grade on it. Worst of all, she had no interest in casting Betty in anything. Betty read for *Our Town* for the role of Emily, but Miss Woodward said that Betty would not be "right" for the part. "Why not? Betty asked. "Well, the point of the play is that Emily is innocent, is it not?" Miss Woodward replied. "Isn't it obvious?"

That hurt. What did Miss Woodward know about Betty's social life? Maybe she heard the school's gossips. Maybe she just watched Betty interact with boys. Betty was a natural flirt, and she knew what boys wanted and what they thought. I told her. She loved hearing about it, and she asked a million questions. Boys would look at her breasts and she'd look at their crotch. A boy would innocently say "How come?" and she'd say "With you." A boy would be kissing her and she would move her own legs apart. Annabelle and Betty could talk about how fast they could get hot and they'd both giggle about how they got a boy hard or how they got a guy to cum before anything could happen. I wasn't sure how many boys/girls were doing things like that, but I do know that Betty seemed to revel in it more. At Tommy's Drive-in, Betty was in her natural element. She could walk there from her house, and she often did after 10:00 PM when she was supposed to be in her room asleep. She could walk over and immediately see guys she knew. Sometimes flirtatious conversations would start on one night and go over a week or so before a boy would have the nerve to ask her to get in his car and go to the bushes. She almost always went. She liked being the aggressor and she liked the attention. She didn't like the "bad reputation" that resulted, and she alternated saying she didn't care about it to swearing that she was going to stop. She never stopped.

At school she wasn't so open, but she had the most expressive eyes God ever granted a teenager. She could undress a guy with a look. She could make off color comments with a glance. She could ridicule a teacher with a raised eyebrow. She could convey the hurt of the ages with a downcast stare. And she could mock another girl's feigned prudishness with the widest eyes in West Texas. Smiles, frowns, postures and furrowed brows were also in her arsenal but her eyes always stole the show. Miss Woodward, as they say in West Texas, wasn't buying what Betty was selling, however. Miss Woodward had also mastered the hardened stare and she would pull the oldest trick in the teacher's book. "Betty, you seem to have something to say. Why don't you say it for us all to hear?" Betty could not intimidate her by roaming her eyes to parts of Miss Woodward's body below the waist the way she could a male teacher. Woodward would wait, "Well, Well, do you have something to say?" "No Ma'am," was Betty's only response and only defense. Among the girls, Annabelle was her only ally anyway, and Annabelle got out of speech and drama after the first semester. Annabelle was a bit more aggressive than Betty in certain ways and certainly a lot more self-confident. "Who cares if that bitch likes me?" said Annabelle, "And who needs her anyway?" Betty did.

Speech and theater, especially theater, were Betty's life. Like a million before her and a million after her, she thrived on losing herself on stage. There she could be someone else, a virtuous heroine, a black-hearted witch, or a rabbit. It didn't matter to her. Her parents did not push her to perform or be on stage, quite the contrary. Her mother was tolerant of it and her dad was more or less oblivious to it except to criticize the moral values of actors. He prohibited her from going to movies on Sunday (a prohibition, oddly enough, she obeyed) and he specifically disliked her seeing particular movies (e.g. anything with Elvis Presley). But for as long as I could remember she was fascinated with acting, movies and stars. She had movie magazines that she hid as effectively as I hid first Swedish "health" magazines and then Playboy. She also acted for me, for her friends and in playful ways with her sisters and brother. She pretended to be people, things, and animals. For me she was Eddie Cantor with a dress, but later I thought she was more like Carol Burnett and then ultimately I decided she was in fact Shelley Long [well, she looked like Shelley Long and then there is that name, Shelley]. She loved to act, and back in her bedroom on many occasions I was treated to everything from the Munchkins to whatever Natalie Wood had done last. During Betty's seventeenth year I saw Betty do both bits of *Splendor in the Grass* and "I Feel Pretty" from *Westside Story*. Oddly enough I never saw her perform on stage since I was at the other school across town, and she never, as far as I know, saw me play baseball or football. Mine was the greater loss.

While I never saw her on stage, I certainly heard about her trials and tribulations with Miss Woodward. From her early worries about how she'd get along with the new teacher to the agony of never being cast for a play her senior year, I heard about it all. Not being selected for the spring play, *Winterset*, hit Betty very hard. She wanted a particular part, Margo, and she wanted to go out of OHS with a "blaze of glory." She didn't get the part, of course. In addition, her boyfriend, Mack, got a major part. He was to play Trock, a cold-blooded killer who had no remorse for his victims. Mack had never done a play before but his dark and brooding good looks made Miss Woodward think of him as a perfect killer. Besides Mack was smart and he learned quickly. Betty would settle for stage manager where she could work closely with the actors, provide them tips, and be close to Mack. But it killed her not to have a part. She ranged from being furious at Miss Woodward to worrying that she was not really good enough to hoping that the play would bring her and Mack back together. Mostly she was upset that her theater life and her personal life were collapsing simultaneously.

Betty did not tell me everything about her relationship with Mack. Some of it I simply assumed, like that they were having sex. She did tell me about the turmoil they had in that last year. Mack broke up with her more than once. It was one of those on again and off again romances, for sure. I understood, I had one myself, but hers seemed more, well, dramatic. She "cheated" on him, but he would not "really" take her out. She saw him with another girl. He saw her talking to a "thug" at Tommy's. She could not stop thinking about him. He could not stop calling her at night. They fought and they made up. They made up and they fought. I really saw nothing unusual about it since it paralleled my own relationship and the relationships of everyone else I knew. The level of emotion in Betty's retelling of her senior year did exceed anyone else's, but then that was Betty. Admittedly I felt for her more about the play. That was so important to her, and she was so good. I felt she deserved it and that she had earned it. I didn't much like Mack anyway since he would never take her out in public. He took another girl to the prom, for God's sake.

Then and now it struck me as curious that Miss Woodward chose to *Winterset* as the senior play. It is a semi-famous play, of course, but take another look at it and put it in the context of Odessa, Texas in the early '60s as performed by high school kids. Maxwell Anderson had radical tastes in both theater and politics. The play is written in blank verse. Anderson wrote it in the mid '30s at the height of the depression and he clearly meant *Winterset* to be at least a partial indictment of either capitalism or capitalists or both. It is based on a true story of the Sacco-Vanzeti case of perhaps wrongly accused Italian radicals and one of their son's attempt to revenge the miscarriage of justice that led to their execution. The son fifteen years later searches for the truth and encounters the unpleasantness of American society and American justice. The play is heavy and at times heavy-handed. Few kids knew about the original story of Sacco and Vanzetti or understood the significance of their case in American history. Among their parents, those who did know the story probably wished there were some way to have them executed twice! Evidently none of this occurred to Miss Woodward, and as a result of Betty's death, she lost her Trock. The play did not go on. I can't help thinking that in some ironic way, Betty may have saved Miss Woodward's job at OHS. But perhaps not enough people would have seen it or understood it anyway.

Betty loved the play. She wanted to be part of it and she wanted it to be successful. She committed herself wholeheartedly to making it a success. At some point in early to mid-March, 1961 she began to act more depressed and sadder, and according to numerous kids working with the play, she asked many of them to kill her. She had told me about how upset she was with not being in the play and how Mack had broken her heart. She never told me that she had asked people to kill her, and she never told me specifically that she asked Mack to kill her. It's true that I did not know everything about her life. I did not know about many of her other friends or about her job at Woolworth. I did not know about some creep she befriended who took "credit" for robbing a Cabel's Minute Market. There was a Betty I didn't know. I do know this. She wanted what we all want—to be totally unique while being completely accepted.

Chapter XI
Pretty Little Pet Claudette

"Roy Orbison is a genius," said Betty.

We were sitting in my "candy green" '53 Olds at Tommy's, an oasis of conversation in a vast landscape of hyperactive teens. We sat there for an hour as she nursed a cherry coke and I munched on steak-fingers and drank coke after coke.

"Oh, come on," I responded, "He's a geek who sings funny. Did you hear his latest, *Crying*? I hate it when guys sing high like that."

"It's called falsetto, Shell, and that's the song I am talking about. It's sheer poetry."

"Poetry*?*" I responded, "Roy Orbison is a poet? I guess that would make *Oobie Doobie* and *Pretty Little Pet Claudette* his early sonnets, huh?"

"Poetry is communicating emotion through words, Shelly Belly," said Betty. "Roy is still finding himself through his music, but he's a poet. You'll see."

This was too much for me. Like all teenagers in the late '50s and early '60s music was very important to me. We waited anxiously for KOSA radio to announce the new top ten list every week and we developed strong attachments to our favorite artists. While Buddy

Holly's death had hit me hard in 1959, I mostly favored and argued the merits of black musicians above all others. Chuck Berry, Bo Diddley, and especially Ray Charles were my geniuses. My friends preferred Elvis, Jerry Lee Lewis, and even Roger Miller, *dang me*. Betty liked the one hit wonder, Gogi Grant, Connie Francis, Doris Day, and, oddly enough, Roy Orbison. Orbison was small time and besides that he was from Odessa, or just outside of Odessa anyway.

"He's ugly, Betty Jean," I argued. She was sitting a respectable distance from me in the front seat, but my declaration of Roy's physical appearance made her turn, slide toward me, and swat me on the upper arm

"What does that have to do with anything?" she almost shouted. Then she sat back, thought a second, and then said: "No, wait, maybe that is why he knows pain so well. Because he doesn't look like a thick-headed, burr cut, knuckle-dragging football player, he probably has experienced the pain of rejection and ridicule that West Texans are so skilled at. We are the friendliest people in the world... as long as you act, think, and especially look exactly like all the rest of us."

"Rejection?" I responded. "Are you kidding me? Do you even know Claudette Frady? She's beautiful. No matter what you say, I still don't understand how a guy like him could get such a girlfriend if he's so used to rejection."

I hated dumping on Roy Orbison. I actually liked the guy quite a lot. For many years he had been bringing his baby blue Cadillac into my Dad's car wash at least once a week. He called me "Kid" and I called him Mr. Orbison. He was always alone, usually very quiet, and unfailingly polite. While he was not classically handsome, he was in fact charismatic. He also dated and eventually married Claudette Frady, better known to all of us as Billy Frady's big sister. When Betty and I lived on Muskingum Street, the Frady family lived three houses north of Betty and four houses north of me. When we all stunned when Roy sold *Pretty Little Pet Claudette* to the Everley brothers for the flip side of one of their big hits,

All I Have to Do Is Dream. Still my sixteen-year old mind could not comprehend how Roy could get a pretty girl friend. When a starting quarterback, a total jerk, got a pretty girl, it made sense, but not when a geek got one.

"He's gentle, Shell, and he has beautiful eyes," Betty explained. She went on: "I can't be sure, but like all great poets, all great writers, I am sure he accepts life as a mystery. He has deep insight. He probably makes his girl feel important in unraveling all life's mysteries."

"Hmmm, that may appeal to you, but that's not what I see around me," I said. "Girls like tall, strong, confident idiots for the most part. Just look out the window, Betty Jean. Look at 'em."

In truth my case was made right there. Sitting in adjacent cars, walking to and from Tommy's dining room, and cruising past us were couples and groups of kids matched up by looks alone. To be a "cute couple" in Odessa meant to be physically matched.

Betty looked at the kids and thought about what I had said. Then she shot back: "You're right for the most part, Shell, but look at you. Excuse me, but you aren't tall and you sure aren't stupid and you have girlfriends."

"But I am a football player and look at you. Are you dating a poet?" I asked. "Last time I looked, you were dating a tall football player. And unlike Roy Orbison, he doesn't wear glasses and it doesn't look like someone put out a fire on his face with a track shoe."

"Leave Mack out of this! You don't know Mack. No one really knows Mack!" Her tone was anxious and insistent suddenly, and I knew I could not press too much.

"Betty Jean, I am not criticizing Mack. You're right. I don't know him at all. But you go on and on about poets and actors and you say you hate football, but here you are dating a football player."

She slid across the seat, turned her back to the door and pulled her knees up to her chin. For a second, she just sat there staring at me. Then she asked:

"Are all players on your team exactly alike?" She didn't wait for an answer. "You're different and that cute Jack Littlefield with the big vocabulary is different, too. Well, so is Mack."

"How so?" I wondered.

"He's sensitive. He's lonely even when he is with people. But most of all he's a listener."

"Huh? What does that mean?" I asked.

She knew I wasn't that dumb. "I mean he listens to me," she said. "He listens to me and he asks about me. Other than you, Shell, he's the only guy in this whole god-forsaken town who listens to anyone except himself."

"OK," I said, "so he listens to you, but what is he thinking about you? How can you know he really cares for you?"

"He does care for me," she said. "He tells me he does, and he acts like he does."

I turned and looked at her all scrunched up against the passenger-side car door. "Then why won't he take you out in public?"

That instantly jolted her back to an upright position. She shot back at me: "Excuse me, do you live in Odessa, Texas? Do you know how this town is? Can a football player date a nobody at OHS? Maybe at your precious Permian, but not at OHS." She was not pretending to be upset. This was the real deal.

She had a point, but so did I, and I was not going to be deterred.

"Well, if he can't be seen with you, is he thinking about himself or you and your feelings?" There was only one answer to that. Logic was on my side.

"Oh, hush, Shell. You have never been in love. You have to make sacrifices for love. I am in love right now, totally and utterly and, I repeat, you don't know him."

"Here's what I know, Betty Jean," I said. "I hate it that he won't be seen with you and handsome or not, I don't like his looks."

That shocked her. "Why is that, Shell, why?" She cared what

I thought.

"He's tall, thin, and has jet black hair," I said, thinking that I had made an obvious point.

"So?" she responded.

"That's the Williams' look, and you know it," I said. "Your dad, my dad, Grandpa Pete, and all the brothers. It's the classic Williams' look."

"You're horrible, Shell, just horrible. Go away and leave me alone." She started pushing me with her feet against the car door. She was literally kicking me out of my own car. Her tears and her emotions were real, so I opened the door and nearly fell out. I had just done a terrible thing.

I had just accused Betty of falling in love with her father.

CHAPTER XII
Fight! Fight!

Odessa always had a reputation for violence. Newcomers in the '50s were told lurid stories about bar fights and shootouts from the old days, but in truth the '50s were as wild and wooly as any time that preceded them. The saying that "Midland is where you raise your kids and Odessa was where you raise your hell" was true. Midland, twenty miles and seemingly light years away, was corporate oil. The owners, financiers, and managers lived there, while the roughnecks lived in Odessa. Midland was the "Tall City," while Odessa was ...well, Odessa was laid out with no seeming regard for zoning or aesthetic impact. On Grant Street, downtown, a mile stretch saw a beer joint, an empty lot, a church, a music store, someone's house, a small grocery, and so on. The legendary Slim Gabrel, elected sheriff in 1956, is widely credited with "cleaning up" Odessa. Mostly that consisted of moving the hookers indoors and busting the most public displays of drunkenness and bad behavior. What happened behind closed doors or after midnight didn't much change. Gangs and racial conflict lay the future, and organized crime had bigger fish to fry in Dallas.

The average citizen in Odessa did not much encounter

violence on a daily basis by the late '50s. City streets were safe, and all the attributes of civil society were in order. Baptist churches were everywhere and so were the Methodists. Presbyterians, Lutherans, and even Catholics had places of worship. Rotary, Jaycees, and Kiwanis were all in place. "The Globe Theater," a replica of the original, featured well done Shakespearean drama. There was a symphony orchestra. And then there were the schools: OHS, Permian, Blackshear, Ector High Schools and Odessa Junior College, founded in 1946. Odessans loved the place and took great pride that West Texans were the "friendliest" people in the world. There was certainly respectable society in Odessa and the notion that Odessa was in anyway inferior to Midland, Dallas, or New York would be "fightin' words."

Teenagers in Odessa reflected the fierce individuality of their parents and believed even more intensely in the cosmic value of the little piece of desert they happened to be occupying. Why would anyone, ever, want to live somewhere else or even visit there? Going to Midland to take a date to Luigi's Italian Restaurant might be about as "uptown" as any of them ever dreamed of. To feel completely superior, to get a bargain, or to get laid, they might venture to El Paso to step across the border to Juarez, Mexico, but that was about it. What parents generally didn't know, especially the moms, was that their kids from junior high and above in the mid-to-late '50s faced the daily prospect of violence in their lives. Bonham Junior High was an example. In 1957 thirteen and fourteen year old boys came to school not knowing if that day they would be dragged into the "thug-football boys" battle for territorial supremacy at Bonham. Richard Thomas, a thug who had been in a juvenile delinquent's home, reputedly started it. He was nineteen, and he confronted "pretty boy" football player Kenneth Benson in the school parking lot. Thomas verbally humiliated Benson and taunted him. Then he hit him twice in the face. To keep Benson from going down, Thomas stepped on Benson's foot, so he wouldn't fall when he hit him.

For the following two weeks at Bonham, a fight between

thugs and football boys broke out every day. The thugs looked distinctively different from the crew cut, button down football boys, but race was not a factor. Everyone was white. The "bad-ass thugs" had ducktail haircuts, wore black leather jackets, and pointy-toed shoes. They "cheated" when they fought. They kicked a guy in the nuts or they carried switchblade knives. There were no particular leaders or particular gang-like structures, but they intended to intimidate the football boys as a class of people and show them who was boss. No one asked any sociological or psychological questions about this conflict. And no one told his parents. They just went to school and survived. Occasionally a thug and a football boy would square off and fight in the schoolyard. Once or twice three thugs would corner a football boy in the boy's bathroom. Once a bunch of football boys went to the school's wood-cutting shop to get handy pieces of wood to use as clubs. The wood-shop teacher, an Assistant football coach, looked the other way. Once or twice kids were followed home by a carload of the opposite group.

It all came to a head on a Friday. The two groups agreed to meet in the school gym. They put boards through the door handles to lock them from the inside, and then they started to rumble. Fists, chairs, clubs, and at least one knife were the weapons of choice. The fight seemed to last for an eternity but the clock suggested that it took only fifteen minutes. The football boys won that fight. They knocked the thugs down or out and they kicked them as they lay there. Most of the thugs got up and ran away, but Ronnie Grammar, one of the big thugs, got only as far as the football locker room before Jimmy McClendon caught up with him. Ronnie was 17, slow mentally, and hostile. Jimmy was 15 and as tough as they come. Jimmy charged Ronnie, but Grammar was able to cut the middle linebacker from his wrist to his elbow with a switchblade knife. Football Coach Jim Daniels, a World War II Pacific campaign veteran, came into the locker room ten seconds after Jimmy fell. He looked at the frightened Grammar and the bleeding McClendon and he said what any caring, concerned educator would normally say:

"Try to use that knife on me you big son-of-a-bitch and I'll ram it up your ass!" That fight did not end the rivalry, but the thug-football boy conflict never again involved large numbers of combatants.

Nearly every Friday or Saturday night somebody had a fight in Odessa, however. Guys would be standing around Tommy's, one guy would smart off to another, harsh words would be exchanged, and then one would shove the other. They wouldn't fight at Tommy's. Instead someone would yell "fight, fight" and they would form a convoy of cars, ride out to the edge of town on the edge of a pump jack, circle the cars, and use the eerie glow of the headlights to illuminate the featured bout. Reputations rose and fell with these clashes. Some guys looked for the chance to kick the shit out of the latested reputed bad ass in town; others hoped they'd never have to be in that circle of lights from which few emerged unbloodied. Sometimes the fights just made no sense. One night Butch Goliad saw someone drive away from his car in a green Ford. He threw a rock into the side of the car and hit it hard. Whoever was driving that car had stolen his back two hubcaps. He drove to Tommy's and waited next door to the drive-in in the Junior College parking lot until a green Ford with a dent in its side drove around. He then chased the Ford down Andrews Highway and then up 27th street until he could cut it off. By the time his friends from Tommy's could catch up with him, Butch had hoisted the driver of the Ford on the back of his own car. Butch held the guy's shirt in his left hand while he pummeled the presumed hubcap thief with a tire tool. Unfortunately, there were no hubcaps, stolen or otherwise, in the guy's trunk. Just another Saturday night in Odessa.

Permian High School was nothing like Bonham Junior High, even though the vast majority of kids attending Permian had gone to Bonham. The halls and bathrooms were safer. Few fights broke out in the parking lot. Even the guys who had been thugs at Bonham seemed calmer at Permian. Of course, there was no question where the football boys stood in the social order. They and their girlfriends won every elected office, every award, and everyone's heart. Or so it seemed. The band was one of the best in state from the day the school opened, and speech and debate teams were stellar. OHS was the same. Its halls were safe, clean, and noisy. If the '50s had a Happy Days reputation, most of the kids at these two schools would say their high schools deserved it. The town was growing; the schools were thriving; the oil was flowing; and even though Buddy Holly had died, the music was the best ever. Very few of the boys went to high school that year or the year after expecting a fight. Was this what "normal life" was supposed to be like?

Tommy's

-- Mike King

Chapter XIII
You Just Don't Understand

Mary Belle Williams spoke in hushed tones. "Betty Jean, you just have to put such notions out of your head. Your father won't have you carrying on like that."

"Like what?" Betty said. "It's just a job at respectable store. Woolworth is a great place. As good as Penney's!"

"That's not the point, Honey, and you know it," said Mary Belle. "Working late on Saturday nights and working every other Wednesday, you'll start missing church. I know you missed last Wednesday when Daddy was sick. Preacher mentioned it yesterday at prayer circle."

"Good Grief, Mama, what is this, Communist Russia? I can't even miss one night 'cause I am bloated and gassy from cramps!"

"Elizabeth! Watch your language, young woman!"

At that very point, Joe came through the kitchen door. Betty knew instantly that there was big trouble ahead. He had "that look." Williams' men had a way of furrowing the brow, tightening the muscles around the mouth, holding their bodies in a curious way that was both aggressive and pitiful, and simply looking at you as if you had just insulted their sainted mother. Under no circumstances would they speak first when they had "the look." It was an absolute imperative for you to ask, preferably with a concerned tone "Oh,

Daddy, what's wrong?" And that literally means "What have I done now?"

Betty would usually try not to say it, but she could never make it. Eventually she'd give in. We all did. All Williams' children did. It was an absolute imperative. This time she didn't wait. Might as well get it over with. She'd rather face his anger than his morose posturing.

"Daddy, what is it?" Betty asked. Curiously neither Betty nor I ever worried that one of our fathers would confront us with something really serious from an objective perspective. She didn't fear getting caught sneaking out and I never worried about staying out all night while my mother fretted about my safety. No, what we got in trouble for was the subtle thing--the attitude, the unintended wound to their egos, a slight misstatement, a lack of appreciation for all they had done for us. Anything that lessened their hold over us was the impetus for hours of crying, harsh punishment, or guilt-inspiring put downs. My dad threatened to sell the car wash and cut my mother and me off financially once because he thought that I showed too much happiness that rain had closed the rack one Saturday and I didn't have to work. I was ten years old at the time. Joe would pull the same emotional blackmail on Betty for not being excited enough about a certain sermon, for not wanting to listen to his stories rather than listen to "bebop" on the radio, or for wearing a certain dress that he didn't care for. Usually, it was the little thing, but this time it was different.

"Sister, don't I care for you and this family?"

"What?" Oh shit, here we go again, she thought. "Of course," said Betty.

"Then why do you want to leave? Why did you send off for an application to Indiana University?" said Uncle Joe.

"Did it come? Is it here? Did they accept me?" Betty asked excitedly. "They have a great drama school. It is close to our old home. I want to get out of this town." Betty spurted out reasons that had nothing to do with getting away from her dad, her reputation, or her troubles with Mack.

"It came, but it's gone now. I threw it away. You can't leave this family, our home, and the church. You belong right here. Don't your ever think of anyone but yourself?"

"Yes, of course, but…"

Betty knew not to argue. I knew not to argue. Her sisters, except for Tricia occasionally, and her brother at that time did not argue. Her mom did not argue. More protestations would only mean more hurtful statements, a threat to leave, or like my dad, a feigned heart attack. Arguing would lead to more restrictions, maybe a public prayer at church on the agony she causes her father, or perhaps an outburst of name calling that would hurt all the more because Betty herself believed the names to be accurate. She had learned that only one response to his hurt could make him stop. She left the room crying, knowing that her mother would reassure him that Betty was only emotional because it was "her time of the month." That was the way in our family. Leave the big issues unresolved. Let dad bully and distort. Never tell the truth.

Soon, Mack would kill her.

CHAPTER XIV
Kiss and Kill

Life went on after Betty died. Permian hosted the state-wide Student Council annual conference that very week-end. I was the official greeter. As busloads of kids would come into the parking lot, I would jump aboard to smile, wave, and tell them "howdy" from all the friendly folks in West Texas. I did it. Baseball games were not canceled. I played. Classes continued. I went. Many times in my life after that I would be told by my family, my school, or my government to "carry on with daily activities as normal." I could always draw on my experiences in March and April of 1961 to do so. The numbness one feels allows it, but a few seconds of every hour it doesn't seem right.

My friends never knew the bond between Betty and me. Everyone had problems at home and dads always seemed to be the reason. This one died. That one drank. Another one hit his kids or his wife. Most suffered the booms and busts of the oil business in some fashion or another. A rich kid in elementary school was poor in junior high, rich again the sophomore year, and then busted as a junior. For the most part, moms didn't work outside the home. They were highly visible and highly supportive, but they didn't work at outside jobs. Betty's family was poorer than most, and her mom worked as a sales clerk at Penney's. What really seemed to make us different was that our dads were masters of psychological manipulation. To the outside world they were earthy and garrulous charmers. We were their first children. Nothing we did could satisfy them. Her dad hated theater, and my dad hated football. My dad wanted me at the car wash every waking moment. Her dad wanted her at church more than that. My dad constantly threatened to leave my mom and me because I had hurt him so much for not wanting to work more or for wanting to go to college to study political science. Betty's dad more than once talked of suicide. They both thought Odessa Junior College would be just fine but Betty and I dreamed of big universities in far away places.

Betty and I talked on the phone, in the car on holidays, and whenever we saw each other at Tommy's. I had no brothers or sisters, but Betty was close. The Christmas before she died we talked about Mack. He had broken up with her, and her life was shattered. She had contemplated suicide; in fact she had even tried it with four aspirin. Huh? Four aspirin wouldn't kill you. It might cure a really bad headache. "No," she laughed, "but it upset my stomach." She wasn't laughing and joking about the relationship with Mack, but she seemed even more disturbed about the new drama teacher at OHS than she did Mack. Betty had applied to Indiana University for their theater department, and the new teacher just didn't like her. She wasn't casting her in anything, and it might hurt Betty's chances at IU. Neither of us knew if our fathers would let us go to college away from Odessa. They were not educated men, and they did not respect their eldest children's goals. Eventually Betty would die to get away. When my dad found that I would go to the University of Texas to study political science (called Government there), he kicked me out of the house and refused to pay my tuition the four years I was there. Suicide never entered my mind.

Did it really enter Betty's? She had talked about it. She had once or twice caused a stir at OHS by acting like she was going to do it. She was full of self-loathing. She found her own behavior unacceptable one minute and bragged about it the next. She really did love Jesus. I put her talk of death and suicide into the context of our family history. We were a dramatic lot. Every one of the males craved attention at all times. Betty was like the males in that regard. She wanted to be on that stage, and self-pity was her gimmick. She was thin and pretty; she had a nice smile; and she had real acting talent. My excuse for not telling anyone that she was contemplating death and suicide was that it just didn't seem that remarkable to me. She wasn't "joking," but she wasn't serious. My mother told me that when her dad, my Uncle Joe, lived with her and Daddy, he threatened suicide often, usually in the middle of the night. My mother would get up and sit with him at the table and talk until the sunshine came in the kitchen window. Finally he did it once too often. Mama told him to go ahead and do it. She'd clean it up in the morning. Daddy had always pretended to be sleeping when all this occurred, but when she said that to Joe, he looked up from the sheets and said: "Finally"! They both rolled over and went back to sleep, and the following morning Joe acted like nothing had ever happened. Did Betty really want to die?

Communication with my aunt and uncle almost completely stopped after Betty died. Neither of them ever asked me a single question about Betty or the allegations that surfaced about her. Forty years later and they still haven't. Perhaps they knew all they needed to know; perhaps they didn't want to know. It never occurred to me that Betty's hopes and fears would ever be relevant to anyone but her. Even after she died, I didn't think so.

Betty's funeral was my first experience with death or its attendant rituals. Her killer's trial was to be the first real encounter I was to have with the American justice system. Perry Mason was all I had to go on. At 16 I thought it would be an open-and-shut case, but from day one surprises awaited us all. Betty had been shot. Mack Herring did it because she had asked him to do so. She had written a note absolving him of all responsibility, but the note was

81

not released to the press. John Sliney, a local reporter for the Odessa American, was actually at the scene when Mack dragged Betty's body out of the stock pond. Other reporters were there as well, and all of them were allowed to ask Mack questions both at the pond and back at the Winkler County jail. Sliney asked the calm and self-possessed boy why he had done it. His reply was "I don't know. I guess I am crazy." The American and many other papers state and nation-wide carried the story on the front pages for a couple of days. It was immediately tagged "The Kiss and Kill Murder." The trial was not until the following February. Both the trial and the newspaper ignored the subject of the "Kiss and Kill Murder" until then. They missed a lot.

High School Youth Shows Officers Girls Body In Stock Pond
Suspect Relates Plans Of Slaying

Betty Williams

Headlines from Odessa American Archives

CHAPTER XV
Happy Fourth

In the late '50s, early '60s in West Texas high school kids went on dates. If you wanted to know someone better or if you just wanted to spend time talking to that person, you asked her out on a date. The answer might be, what about next weekend? I have a date with Harry this weekend. Some kids had a date with a different boy/girl every weekend. Sometimes you ended up in the bushes making out, sometimes you didn't. A large number of couples went steady, exchanged football jackets and heart chains broken in half, but as many just played the field. Betty didn't get to date like other kids. Her parents thought it was because she worked too hard and went to church so often. To a certain extent they thought she was a "normal" teenager. She wasn't. She had a reputation. No one would take her out in public. As a "popular" football boy, I did go on dates when I wasn't with my more or less steady girlfriend Jennifer Johnson. Jenny went to OHS. We had an on again, off again relationship, and in 1961, it was off again early in the summer.

That meant that when I wasn't working at my Dad's car wash or playing baseball I went on dates or hung out at Tommy's. Mack Herring was everywhere that summer. I once saw him walk out of Tommy's dining room, come across the lot toward his car, and then pantomime a death scene as one of his buddies pretended to shoot him. A couple of weeks later I was on a date with Callie Lewis. We already had our steak fingers and cherry cokes on a tray hung on the driver-side window when Mack and a date pulled in beside us. I looked up to see Mack rolling down his window. With a big smile, he waved at me and said, "Hey, Shell, how's it hanging"? I unhooked the tray and let it fall to the ground and backed out. Tommy never said a word to me about the mess. He relaxed his strict behavior code on my behalf. Twenty-five years later he told me that he would have relaxed his no fighting rule, too, had I chosen to attack Mack. At that point I had no intention of fighting Mack or provoking him to attack me. That would change before the summer was out.

By the Fourth of July, Jenny and I were back together again. JJ, as I called her, was excited because she had been invited to one of the popular girls' Fourth of July parties. Going to an OHS party was fine with me. I had gone to the junior prom there with her. I knew everyone and I had played sports with and against every one of the boys. The party was essentially boring for me since the OHS kids seemed a lot more cliquish than Permian kids, but I also speculated that they weren't as comfortable with my presence as I assumed they would be. Mack was there. He stayed on his side of the backyard, and I stayed on mine. He was loud. I told JJ that I didn't want to be at the same place at the same time as Mack, but she told me simply to ignore him. She didn't talk to him or anything, so if I turned my back, I could pretend he wasn't there. Around 10:30 PM, I heard a series of firecrackers go off followed by a burst of giggles. When I turned to see what was going on, I couldn't believe my eyes. Mack was chasing girls with firecrackers. He'd light three or four at a time and then throw them at a girl or set of girls. They would laugh and run away. As the West Texas saying goes, "I am a lover, not a fighter, but I know what's worth fighting over."

I had to leave. I could not hit him with all his OHS friends around. They would gang up on me. I couldn't stay. I couldn't ignore his antics, the girls' giggles, or the whole group's collective shunning. They would not talk to me because I was Betty's cousin. They had no condolences for me. They had nothing for me. JJ wouldn't go, couldn't go. She had struggled to "make it" at OHS and this was her breakthrough. She had gone to Bonham Junior High, not Bowie or Crockett like most OHS kids, and she was dating a Permian boy. She couldn't storm out. I was not understanding. Either come with me or that's it. That was it. A year later we briefly reconnected, but we were finished.

My senior year, I met the girl who became my wife. That girl, Janell Hollis, was outraged by Betty's death, and at first she didn't know Betty was my cousin. I saw JJ only once my senior year. Our football coach, Tubby Ted Dawson, stormed into our locker room just prior to our game with OHS. Some damned fool was parading in front of the stands with a stuffed Permian Panther with a broad yellow streak down its back. We piled out of the locker room just in time to see my former girlfriend dragging the fake Cat. It was the single best motivator our team ever experienced. Nerves, tension, and anxiety gave away to unadulterated fury. We went out on the football field and kicked OHS' butt from here to Tuesday, as the old West Texas saying goes. Thank you, JJ.

Mack was not in school that year.

Shelly at the July 4th Party

CHAPTER XVI
The Trial

The Winkler County Courthouse in Kermit, Texas, was built in 1929. Its built-in Ionic Greek columns make the building appear more stately than it actually is. The huge square latticed windows and three floor-to-ceiling entry doors suggest majesty and solemnity. Still it seems like an unlikely place to have held the most infamous murder trial in Odessa history. Nevertheless the killing had occurred in Winkler County, not in Ector County. Mack Herring's dad had a hunting lease on a piece of property that sat just outside of Notrees that itself is just inside Winkler County, and the stock pond was on that property. James Waddell, a prominent Winkler County rancher, actually owned the land. Virtually no one in Kermit knew either the boy or the girl, but everyone knew the attorney the Herrings had hired to get their son out of a serious jam.

The defense attorney, Warren Burnett, had not asked for a change of venue. Winkler County was just fine to him and his client. He was certain that he could get a fair trial there. At thirty-five Burnett was already a legend. Dapper, roughly handsome, and clever, he never lost. As a newly minted DA in Odessa he had once won a case that put a young man to death, so for the past few years he had gone over to the other side. He was the finest defense attorney in West Texas. He had tried many a case in Winkler County. Most of the folks who would gather there in February 1962 wanted, by God, to see what Warren Burnett might pull this time. Burnett had pulled many a rabbit out of a hat, but Winkler County jackrabbits were supposedly a different, meaner breed.

Warren Burnett had a reputation. Often he'd come into the courtroom literally seconds before the trial started. Once he did this when he was defending an Odessa man accused of a DWI. Only just then finding out it was a DWI Burnett sat and listened to the state's case. When it came his turn to present witnesses, he called himself as a witness and read his own client's deposition. The case seemed open and shut for conviction. The man had been drinking at the American Legion lodge; he was driving very slowly down the middle of 27th street on the way home at midnight; and the police stopped him, arrested him, and booked him for driving drunk. Burnett read the deposition and seemingly got more and more angry as he read. Finally, he called the arresting officer back to the stand. Then he shocked the judge and everyone else in the room when the asked the patrolman if the Odessa police were concerned more with vengeance or more with justice? The patrolman responded, "Justice, of course." Burnett then asked whether God in punishing Job, therefore, was being vengeful or being just? The patrolman thought a moment about the trick question and then confidently said. "Both."

The judge demanded Burnett to explain the relevance of his unorthodox line of inquiry. It would be obvious "anon," Burnett responded. He then asked the policeman if he in any way gathered any evidence proving that his client was guilty. Did he test his blood, scientifically measure his breath, or make him perform any physical dexterity test? Hearing the policeman say, no, the man was drunk period, Burnett turned and pointed at the stunned cop. "I accuse you of playing God without a license!" Burnett thundered. He turned to the jury. What if his client simply had a beer, but it was in combination with an allergy medicine that made him drive slowly to protect the public's safety? He, Warren Burnett, was certainly not going to tell them that his client in fact took allergy medicine, but the state, which was obligated to prove its case beyond a doubt, could not prove that it wasn't thus. Therefore, the state had not and could not at this time prove beyond a reasonable doubt that his client was drunk because no scientific proof had been presented one way or another. He rested his case with no further witnesses. The jury took ten minutes to find Burnett's client "not guilty." That's how my daddy got out of a DWI in 1959.

The "Kiss and Kill Murder" was no small time DWI case. On Monday morning, February 19, 1962, at 9:00 AM Warren Burnett was on time and he knew what the case was about. G.C. Olsen, a revered and respected jurist in West Texas, presided over the proceedings and he set a business-like tone from the beginning. Dan Sullivan, the DA from Andrews, TX, also in Winkler County, represented the state. He, too, was thirty-five, wore close-cropped hair, and possessed a set jaw. That was the end of his likeness to Warren Burnett, however. He had always been known as a straight-ahead plodder rather a brilliant legal mind. Sullivan had an assistant, John Banks, while Warren Burnett had three. One, Richard Milstead, was from Kermit, and the others were Walter Rogers from Searcy, Arkansas, and Luther Jones from Corpus Christi, TX. For his part, the DA had consistently promised in the press and in private that the outcome of the trial was a foregone conclusion. There was plenty of evidence that Mack Herring had not only committed the crime, he had planned it and carried out the plan to the last detail. It was as obvious case of premeditated murder as one would imagine. He would press for the death penalty.

Burnett opened the proceedings that Monday morning with a move that neither the judge nor the opposing counsel expected. Instead of simply entering a "not guilty" plea for his client, he introduced an affidavit from Mack Herring father, O.L. Herring, swearing that his son, Mack, had been insane at the time of the killing. In short, when he killed that girl, he didn't know what he was doing. Thus, Burnett wished to file a motion for the court to impanel a jury not for a murder trial but rather for a sanity hearing. Burnett proceeded to argue that there would be no dispute of the facts, no dispute that there was planning, and no dispute that his client had been the perpetrator. What was necessary, Burnett said, was for the court to rule on a prior question before a trial could even ensue. The court must first determine whether or not his client was in fact sane or insane at the time of the incident.

Olsen intervened, "Are you saying, Mr. Burnett, that you are pleading 'not guilty on grounds of insanity' for your client?"

No, that was not the case. Burnett reiterated that he wished to file a motion to impanel a jury not for a murder trial but for a hearing on his client's sanity at the time of the killing of Betty Williams. If and only if Mack were found sane would there then be a murder trial. The small crowd gathered there to observe the opening proceedings murmured and mumbled about whether such a thing were even possible! The judge shushed them and looked at Burnett. Burnett was clear-eyed and confident. He knew what the judge was going to ask him and he was ready to answer.

"Mr. Burnett, you understand that in a sanity hearing, the burden of proof is no longer on the state?" the Judge inquired.

"Yes sir, Judge. We'd have it now," said Burnett.

"That's right," the Judge said, "you must prove by the preponderance of the evidence that your client was insane at the time of the shooting."

Warren Burnett had mouthed "by a preponderance of the evidence" as the judge said it. When Olsen said that he had to prove that his client was insane at the time of the shooting, Burnett quickly responded:

"Judge, we are prepared to prove that Mack Herring was insane at the very moment of the shooting."

Veteran lawyers and reporters in the courtroom strained to recall when such a thing had ever occurred. The insanity defense was not new, but was there ever a separate hearing on the sanity of a defendant before the murder trial? They didn't know it then, but the answer to their question was no--it had never been done.

Olsen asked Burnett a couple of more questions to satisfy himself that Burnett knew what he was doing and that he was prepared to present a case. Dan Sullivan, his associate, and the one or two Kermit lawmen in the court were completely taken aback. This was impossible, unprecedented, and ridiculous. The state objected and objected vigorously. Olsen had no choice but to take the lawyers into his chambers to sort through the arguments for and against Burnett's motion. For the next several hours behind closed doors, the lawyers and the judge debated while the stunned onlookers either wandered downtown to the coffee shop, took care of errands, or sat in the nearly empty courtroom discussing the turn of events.

Judge Olsen reconvened the court at 3:30 PM. He announced his decision to grant Burnett's motion. Sullivan strenuously objected, but then he moved for a delay in the hearing for a state-appointed psychiatrist to examine the defendant. The Judge was about to rule favorably on the state's request when Burnett objected.

"Judge, the defendant's sanity now or even before the shooting is not in question" Burnett argued. The defense team would present sound scientific evidence that Mr. Herring was insane at the time of the shooting. The state does not have the burden to prove that he was sane; the defense would have the burden to prove that he was insane. His team would accept that awesome and terrible responsibility.

Judge Olsen thought about Sullivan's request and Burnett's objection. As time stood still, the attorneys waited, Mack Herring leaned forward, the crowd grew completely silent. Judge Olsen took a breath and then he said.

"Request denied. The selection process for the jury for the sanity hearing for Mack Herring will commence in these quarters at 9:00 AM tomorrow morning."

The Imposing Warren Burnett in Court

-- Shel Hershorn

CHAPTER XVII
"Who's Mack?"

By the time the trial started, I was in my senior year. Life had moved on, and so had the interests and concerns of most of the other teenagers. I was consumed with the proceedings, but I was not allowed to attend. Uncle Joe had told my dad that it was best for me to "go on to school" while the trial went on. Its outcome was a foregone conclusion anyway. Daddy wasn't so sure of that because he knew how Warren Burnett operated. He and Warren had partied together, and Burnett had got my dad out of one serious drunk-driving charge. Daddy also had little respect for Dan Sullivan's intellectual capabilities and legal abilities. Sullivan had "shit for brains," according to my dad. He also didn't like what he was hearing from some of his customers at the car wash and the other patrons of the Joker.

The word around town was that Burnett was going to try a "temporary insanity" defense and that it was going to work since Mack Herring, according to just about everyone on the west side of town, was just "not the kind of boy" to kill someone. He was a football boy, not a thug. He was smart, not a mental defective. He had good, church-going parents. He wasn't like one of those juvenile delinquents you'd find in some ghetto in New York City.

One conversation Daddy had really bothered him a lot. A

95

lady customer at the car wash, one who did not know Betty was Bill's niece, told him that "everyone knew that girl was no good, that she tricked him into killing her." He came to me.

"What's she talkin' about, Bill?" My dad didn't like the name Shelly, so he called me everything but that.

Of course, I would never tell my dad anything about the real Betty.

"I have no idea, Daddy. There are always rumors and gossip about kids."

He knew and I knew he knew that I had just confirmed the woman's story.

"You know kids at OHS, don't you?"

"Yes, sir, I do. I know a lot of them."

"Call'em and let's see what we can find out about Mack Herring."

"Why?" I asked.

"Huh, maybe we'll find something that will help Joe or that numbskull Sullivan," he said.

I knew and he knew I knew that wasn't his reason, but I did it anyway. I went to Tommy's and I started talking to kids. It was one of the only times in my life that I ever neglected homework for something else. That is how different I was from Betty, but I was doing this for her, I thought. In a way this book started that night at Tommy's and on the phone a day or two after the trial started.

I met Kay Brownlee and her friend, Janie Andrews, at Tommy's. Kay had dated my buddy, Roland Gladden, and she and I had had a single date. She knew Betty and in fact in the last few weeks of Betty's life, Kay had been important to her. They had a PE class together and Kay, Christian that she was, had befriended this poor soul. Kay even picked Betty for her softball team and it sure wasn't because of Betty's athletic ability. Kay felt like she needed a friend.

"She was a 'messed up' girl, Shell. She asked a bunch of us in PE to kill her," said Kay.

96

"One girl, Andrea, feels just awful because she told Betty to stop asking us and just go do it yourself. Leave us out of it. But, honestly, we didn't think she was serious, just overly dramatic."

"I know," I said, "but what about Mack? What did you think of him?"

Janie broke her silence and blurted: "That cold-blooded SOB!"

I was shocked when Janie said this. I approached a dozen or more kids and called a few others, even JJ, my old girlfriend, and not one OHS kid would say a bad word about Mack. Here an OHS girl did not hesitate.

"I have always thought he was nuts, Shell. A girlfriend used to live on his block and she told me that he'd roam the alleys shooting cats with a .22 rifle. He had a strange sense of humor and I thought he was just creepy. I didn't know him well and I didn't want to know him."

No one else had anything to say about Mack. Betty had told me more. He was sensitive. He liked to hunt and fish. He was smart. Where was the cruel streak that I had seen at Tommy's and at the July 4th party? Did she not notice it? Did she just expect it from boys?

My Permian friends were of no use in this quest. Steve Wilhelm, a really smart guy, was typical.

"He's a murderer, Shell, and they should fry him."

"I know, Steve, but did you know him?" I said.

"No, who the hell knew him? He was a nobody."

No, Betty was nobody. Mack would soon appear in the Odessa American on a daily basis. His dramatic trial would turn him into a "celebrity." His personality and his character would be transformed by a lawyer and by "media coverage." Dell Detective would have a look-a-like on its cover. I had little luck tracking down "dirt" on Mack Herring, but it gave me something to do as the trial and the proceedings unfolded. Through the daily newspaper I became a voyeur in Odessa's "Trial of the Century," I had no idea that Betty, not Mack, would somehow steal the show.

Mack Herring

-- Shel Hershorn

Chapter XVIII
The Hearing

The Mack Herring hearing began on Thursday, February 22 and it lasted three days and three nights. Judge G.C. Olsen told the lawyers presenting the cases that they should be ready to push on to a conclusion, and he told the jurors that he hoped to minimize the disruption in their daily lives as much as possible. Almost two hundred fifty people tried to squeeze into the one hundred-sixty person courtroom. One enterprising young woman stood in the window ledge craning her neck to try to see inside the courtroom as its backdoors stood open to allow the air to circulate. The crowd witnessing the hearing was large, responsive, and at times either shocked or amused. From that first day, both sets of parents, Mack's and Betty's, were there on the opposite front rows. Betty's parents sat alone and somewhat isolated. In the crowded courtroom, they sat on the left side of the room directly behind the DA's table just behind the worn, brown railing separating the lawyers' table from the spectators' gallery. Joe Williams, thin and leathery, looked awkward and uncomfortable in his black suit and white shirt. Mary Belle Williams' long face seemed to have a look of perpetual sadness. She too was dressed in black, but she also wore a cloth green coat from JC Penney's.

On the other side of the aisle, it was a different story. Mrs. Herring's hair, jewelry, and make-up suggested a bit more wealth and breeding than any other woman in the courtroom. Her tailored brown dress may have come from Dallas. Mr. Herring almost vanished in her presence and in looks and dress he could have been Joe Williams' brother. They did not sit alone, however. Sitting beside them on both sides and in two rows behind them were girls, OHS girls, there to support Mack. They were all in dresses and sweaters and many actually wore bobby sox. A few wore red and white OHS football jackets. They were pretty. They were concerned. They could break out in effervescent smiles or well up in tears in a matter of seconds. Most of them and most of the women in the courtroom, including those on the jury, chewed gum. There were no boys. Almost immediately the OHS students were referred to as "Mack's Girls." They were there every minute of every day and every night of the hearing.

In the Odessa American John Sliney reported that Dan Sullivan and his team were shocked and unprepared for Warren Burnett's ploy to convert the proceedings from a trial to a hearing. They had plans to call for a mistrial on that basis alone. Burnett, coy as ever, simply commented that, of course, it had to be a sanity hearing. What other possible approach could his team have taken given the facts of the case? Why shouldn't Sullivan be prepared? Judge Olsen had done the only proper thing. In the war of words played out in the newspaper, Sullivan said that the state would prove that Mack Herring had a motive and that he planned and carried out the murder in a methodical, cold-blooded fashion. Upon hearing Sullivan's statement from a reporter, Burnett smiled and said: "See ya in court."

The jury had been selected the Tuesday before. The eight men and four women picked ranged in age from twenty-seven to sixty-two, and all of them believed in capital punishment. Warren Burnett had not objected to any of them, not even to Mrs. James Waddell, stepmother of the owner of the property on which the death occurred. Of course, Warren had been Warren during the voir dire. He wore an impeccable blue suit and old, what West Texans would call "raggdyassed,"cowboy boots. He smoked unfiltered Camels. He pushed his coat sleeves up to his elbows. And he alternated speaking "good old boy" with quoting Shakespeare and the Bible. He told them that their role would be to do only one thing: to determine whether or not John Mack Herring had been insane at the moment he killed Elizabeth Jean Williams.

The huge crowd, the jury, the dozen or so reporters, and even the DA's team wondered how Burnett would present his case. He had a list of twenty potential witnesses, and it was clear that a huge per cent of them would be "character witnesses." The first one he called was O.L. Herring, Mack's father, but in essence he called none other than Betty Williams herself. Mr. Herring testified that Mack had given his family a letter that Betty wrote the day before she had died. The newspapers had reported the existence of this letter from day one, but only the police and the lawyers knew what it said. Burnett asked Herring to read the letter and in a shaky, emotion-laden voice he did. With his reading of the letter dated March 20, 1961, Betty Williams became a witness for the defense:

> *I want everyone to know that what I am about to do no way implicates anyone else. I say this to make sure that no blame falls on anyone other than myself.*
> *I have depressing problems that concern, for the most part, myself. I am waging a war within myself, a war to find the true me and I fear that I am losing the battle.*
> *So rather than admit defeat I am going to beat a quick retreat into the no man's land of death. As I have only the will and not the fortitude necessary, a friend of mine, seeing how great is my torment, has graciously consented to look after the details.*
> *His name is Mack Herring and I pray that he will not have to suffer for what he is doing for my sake. I take upon myself all the blame, for it lies on me alone.*
> *Betty Williams*

The emotional impact of this letter was lost on no one, but Burnett pressed on with his case. He brought up several high school students to testify that Betty had also asked them to kill her. They were other kids in the play that Mack was in and for which Betty was the stage manager. Burnett also brought in Lacy Turner, the OHS football coach, who praised Mack as a fine young man, a team leader. He came close to saying that he wished all his players were, as people, as good as Mack Herring. He brought in the mother of Mack's current girlfriend. All of the students and all of the adults described Mack as adjusted and normal, above all sane. Betty, however, was morbid and odd. No one took her seriously when she asked them to kill her. She seemed to be joking. That was Betty.

Finally Burnett introduced his star witness. Dr. Marvin Grice was an Odessa psychiatrist. As Burnett questioned him, he laid out an idea that very few people in the courtroom had ever heard of. On the day, in fact the minute, that Mack Herring shot Betty Williams, the teenager was suffering from something called "Gross Stress Disorder." The girl had asked Mack over and over to kill her and the incredible stress from this ordeal had "dethroned Mack of his ability to reason and to act rationally."

Burnett asked: "Did Mack Herring know what he was doing when he shot Betty Williams?"

"No, I don't believe he did," responded Grice.

"Do you believe that he was insane when he shot her?" asked Burnett.

"That is a legal term, not a psychological term, Mr. Burnett, but I do not think the young man was able to discern right from wrong when he shot the girl."

Sullivan tried again to get Judge Olsen to allow a state-appointed psychiatrist to evaluate Herring, but that elicited the same Burnett objection and the same Olsen ruling as it had the two days before. Herring's current mental state was not admissible or relevant. Then Sullivan in his cross-examination began to hammer away at Grice's concept of the stress under which Herring had operated. What exactly is "gross stress disorder"? Korean War soldiers may have suffered it in the midst of combat, the doctor said. What did Betty Williams do that was equivalent to Korean War combat, Sullivan wanted to know? It's not the circumstances; it's the reaction, the Doctor said. Could a person plan such an event and carry it out as planned and still suffer "gross stress disorder" at the moment of the event? Yes, Grice said. Could the boy be expected to live a normal life from this day on? Yes, the Doctor said. Yes.

The afternoon gave way to the evening, a brief dinner break, and then onto the evening as Sullivan interrogated the Doctor. The young DA and then his assistant took turns asking the doctor questions about the disorder and about what Mack could or could not have known while laboring under such a condition. Dr. Grice remained patient, professional, and consistent. Gross Stress Disorder was a real thing; its symptoms were temporary; and Mack Herring had suffered from it. He had seen other teenagers who suffered from it. Judge Olsen listened the best he could, but his body could not deliver what his mind knew to be necessary. He could not pay complete attention and on occasion he would drift off, falling asleep for sometimes a minute or so at a time. When Sullivan finished with Grice, Burnett asked for a redirect. Would the Doctor change his mind on his diagnosis if the DA could prove a motive for the killing? Yes, Grice, said, possibly. Burnett then passed the doctor back to Sullivan, said, "No more questions." At 10:00 PM the day and the defense's witness list was exhausted. Now it was up to Dan Sullivan to present his case, including perhaps a possible motive, against Mack Herring.

On the morning of Friday February 23, Sullivan's approach to the case was clear from the first witness, Sheriff Bill Eddins of Kermit. He had the sheriff recount not only the arrest, the drive to the stock pond, and the retrieval of Betty's body from what Sliney called "her watery grave," he also described Mack's emotional state—"cool as a cucumber." His deputy's report noted that Mack showed little emotion as he went into the stock pond. He lined himself up with two mesquite trees, reached in the water to secure Betty's lifeless form, calmly pulled up the body, and then dragged it to the edge of the water. The deputies and one Texas Highway officer immediately handcuffed Mack and put him in the squad car. They talked to him for fifteen-twenty minutes before turning him over to the reporters. Eddins said that Herring viewed the dead girl's body like he would a "dead cat in the gutter." Even "Mack's girls" reacted to that statement. A reporter in the audience knew that one of the deputies had told him off the record that "I show more emotion taking a crap than that boy did at any time that day." Highway Patrolman, E.C. Locklear, and the deputy, Johnny Stout, were not called and were not at the hearing.

Burnett at first acted as if he had no questions for Eddins, but then he rose.

"Sheriff Eddins, when my client made his comments to you or to your deputies, was a lawyer present? I know I wasn't and none of my colleagues were. Was anyone present?"

"No, sir, it had just happened. We had not even booked him yet."

"Sheriff Eddins, do you or your deputies have Psychology degrees from any of Texas' fine universities"?

"No sir."

"Thank you, Sheriff."

The rest of that day, the state continued to present its case. There was considerable evidence that Mack Herring had planned the event. He had found the lead weights he used to help her sink into the pond at the OHS theater department. He had acquired wire from the Odessa American with which to wrap her dead body and affix the weights. The tracks of his jeep were found at the scene, and so was one of his lace-up boots. The deputies found footprints matching the two kids. One set had them face-to-face at one point. Ike Nail, the boy she had been with when Mack came to get her, was called to testify. He was with Betty, she had been surprised when Mack came, and as she got out of the car to go into his jeep, Betty had said: "I have to call his bluff even it kills me."

By the middle of the evening, Sullivan and his associates

had laid out their case. It was Friday night in West Texas and the largest crowd of the three days had assembled. A large number of them were teenagers. Fred Swanson, the court reporter, sitting to the left of the defense attorney's table, had easily kept up with the proceedings. As the Winkler County Court Reporter for many years, he was familiar with Sheriff Eddins rough grumble, and he knew Sullivan's straight-on "just the facts" style very well. Burnett's dramatic pauses and sometimes rapid-fire questioning had hardly been a factor thus far. The jury box behind Swanson held twelve absorbed jurors who recognized that Sullivan had presented ample evidence to prove that Mack Herring had planned to kill and then had in fact shot Betty Williams. They just didn't know why.

Sullivan then attempted to lay out the possibility that jealousy had motivated Mack. He called a student, Will Rosebud, to the stand. Rosebud had met Betty at a place called Tommy's Drive-In and they had gone out to "the bushes" to talk. Rosebud explained that the bushes just meant that they had driven outside of Odessa to a lonely and excluded area. They had gone out there even though Betty was "seeing" Mack and Mack was Will's friend. Betty had attempted to "disrobe," but Will had told her, no, she was Mack's girl. He told her to put her clothes back on. Sullivan stressed that at the time "last summer" when this occurred Betty and Mack were still "together." In Burnett's cross-examination, he asked the boy what happened when Mack got back. Did they fight? Did they have bad words? Well, no, they talked about it, and then they shook hands, no hard feelings. Perhaps only the teenagers in the room doubted the details of that depiction, but perhaps not.

Judge Olsen had set the pace for the trial but the long hours were beginning to take their toll. His eyes drifted and sagged. Eventually they closed in sleep. In the spectators' gallery, Hazel Locklear whispered to her girlfriend that "that old man should pay attention." Her whisper woke the judge; he peered into the gallery to find the offending party; and various spectators, especially the young ones, found the judge's snoozes and the young woman's whispering thankful relief from the tedious questioning occurring before them. At long last, Sullivan finished. It was nearly 9:30 PM. Everyone was exhausted, but each of them had one question in mind: Would Warren Burnett put Mack Herring on the stand in his own defense or would he just give his closing statement? Old-timers and local lawyers had conflicting views, but none were prepared for what actually happened.

Mack's Girls

-- Odessa American Archives

CHAPTER XIX
The Closing

"Stand up, Mack Herring!" Warren Burnett boomed. "Take the stand!" The long awaited moment had occurred. Mack Herring would testify. This would be the moment of truth, and virtually everyone in the courtroom assumed it would be Warren Burnett's opportunity to shine as well. Warren Burnett would surely guide Herring through an emotional testimony outlining the difficult ordeal the teenager had suffered. Burnett surely would stage-manage the testimony for maximum drama and effect.

Then Burnett said: "I have no questions for this witness, your Honor. I pass him over to my distinguished colleague."

To say that Sullivan was stunned understates the impact of Warren Burnett's move. Sullivan's face registered something between horror and acute appendicitis. Defense attorneys usually don't put their clients on the stand if they don't have to. Defense attorneys don't usually put their clients at the mercy of the DA. Defense attorneys don't usually shift the burden of proof to their client. Warren Burnett was not like most defense attorneys. Dan Sullivan, on the other hand, appeared not to know what to do with the opportunities Burnett presented him. Mack Herring sat before him, but he had not had the luxury of hearing Burnett's questions and Herring's answers. There were no contradictions to exploit and no Freudian slips on which to seize. He was going to have to prove that Herring had a motive or that he was sane at the time of the killing or that he was actually a devious murderer despite the fact that the hearing had supposedly shifted the burden of proof from the state to the defense. And he had to ask a question---now.

Sullivan composed himself and stood up to face the young man. The grave and nervous look on the boy's face did not seem coached or at all faked. How would Sullivan break him down? How would he demonstrate that the kid seethed with anger, resentment, jealousy, rage, or skullduggery?

"When did you first lose touch with reality?" Sullivan asked. Herring answered deliberately but in essence he said he wasn't sure when it happened. At times since and even at the time it all happened, Herring said, he felt like he was in a dream-like state. It was just awful. By the time Herring had described his dreamy, lost-in-a-fog state the night of the killing, it was 10:00 PM and Judge Olsen asked the DA if he could continue the following morning, on Saturday. Sullivan agreed much to the spectators' relief. Everyone assumed that Sullivan could use the break to gather his thoughts and find a more assertive and effective line of questioning to pursue with Herring. Some wondered if either Herring or Sullivan would be able to sleep a wink that night. The whole case would probably come down to one more confrontation, an accused teenager and a determined DA. Warren Burnett would hardly play a role in the next drama to unfold.

On Saturday morning, February 25, everyone was in place --the Judge, the attorneys, Mack's Girls, the spectators and the ever-present press corps. The session opened promptly at 9:00 AM with Dan Sullivan boring in on Mack Herring. Did Herring know that Will Rosebud had dated Betty? Did Mack Herring show remorse for what he had done? Would he do it again? Was it wrong? How long did Betty have to badger him before he was "dethroned of his ability to reason"? How many times did she have to ask? How many minutes did it take? One line of questioning concerned Mack's own social behavior during the summer and fall months of 1961. Had he dated? Was he still going with his girlfriend, Sherry Martin? What was life like as an accused murderer?

Coached or not by Warren Burnett, Mack Herring was a solid witness. He tried to live a normal life since Betty died, and, yes, he had gone out socially a few times. He was still together with his girlfriend and he still had a large circle of friends. He had not been jealous of Will Rosebud, and in fact they had shaken hands at the time Will had taken Betty out. He would not kill again and he knew that it was wrong to have done so, but he thought he was doing the right thing at the time. It was what Betty wanted. He had no idea how he had been dethroned of the ability to reason, how long it had taken, how many times exactly she asked him before losing to ability to reason.

"Let's see," Sullivan said. There was the time at his friend's, Howard Sellars, the time at play rehearsal, an occasion on the way home from play practice, a few more times the next couple of days. Did this sound right to Mack? About right, yes. So maybe six times she asked and maybe for a total of eleven minutes? Maybe, said Mack, I didn't add it up. I didn't count. "You are about the most popular football player in Odessa, aren't you, Mack?" Mack did not respond, but he did not break either. He was sad for what had happened and he would never do it again. That's for sure.

And then it was over. Sullivan kept Mack Herring on the stand for most of the morning, and he hammered away at the timing issue, but he never broke the kid or made him blurt out in anger or frustration. There were no more witnesses after Mack Herring. After the lunch break, Judge Olsen asked the attorneys if they had any more testimony to present but each declined. In essence Warren Burnett's case had started with Betty Williams (as heard in her letter) and had ended with Mack Herring. Now he had the opportunity to address the jury first in his closing statement.

We have before us a simple but tragic matter. A

disturbed and confused young woman with a death wish prevailed upon a young man who had once been her boyfriend to do her biding by taking her life. In her own words we have heard the girl exonerate the young man from her death. Should he have done so? Of course not. Would he ever do such a thing again? Again, of course not. A distinguished psychiatrist has explained to us how Mack Herring, operating under this great pressure, lost his ability to reason when confronted with this ultimate appeal. This was not a normal request. It was not under normal circumstances. The incredible pressure of this extraordinary request got to the young man. He was not thinking clearly or properly, but he also was not thinking about himself. He had nothing to hide, nothing to cover up. He had no anger or malice of forethought. He simply wanted to help his former girlfriend unburden herself from all the stresses in her young life. As Dr. Grice told you sitting right here in this witness chair, young people often crack under this kind of pressure. It is just too much. They can no longer think clearly. Soldiers, policemen, and other adults sometimes even crack under this pressure. It is called "Gross Stress Disorder." If our finest citizens can yield to this disorder, who are we to say that a teenager cannot? If our finest citizens can at once crack but then recover to live perfectly normal lives, who are we to say that this teenager cannot?

Ladies and Gentlemen, you are going to be asked a single question: "Was the defendant capable of telling right from wrong when he killed Betty Williams?" Not before or after he killed her, but at the time he killed her? The evidence and Dr. Grice's testimony provide the only possible answer to this question. No, he could not. That must be your answer as well. No, the defendant, John Mack Herring, that boy sitting over there next to his mother, that boy did not know right from wrong when he tragically, in the rational mind, inexplicably, killed Betty Williams. That, Ladies and Gentlemen, is the only rational explanation in this puzzling situation. The honorable District Attorney could offer no clear alternative to the Doctor's diagnosis. The Doctor himself said that the articulation of a clear and compelling motive would even make him change his assessment of Mack Herring's ability to reason at the time of the killing, but you have sat here with me for three days and three nights. Have you heard of such a motive? Has there been a clear explanation? Is there an alternative to the obvious? No, John Mack Herring could not tell right from wrong when he killed Betty Williams. That is the determination that you must now confirm in your deliberations, Ladies and Gentlemen. Do your duty.

Dan Sullivan addressed the jury next. As he spoke, Warren Burnett lit a cigarette. As Sullivan presented his closing argument, Burnett smoked while the ash on the cigarette grew longer and longer. Soon there was more glowing ash than cigarette. It was an old lawyer's trick, but it worked. Burnett had placed a straight pin through the length of his cigarette, so it held the ash for as long as Burnett took drags on it. The jury members could not help noticing the precarious ash's improbable growth. Sullivan, unaware of Burnett's tactical distraction, plodded on.

Ladies and gentlemen, my esteemed colleague and I agree on one important item. This case involves a tragedy. Two teenagers, once lovers, got caught up in an intrigue in which one of them died. There is no disputing what happened. John Mack Herring killed Betty Williams. He admits it and he admits planning it. For two days more or less, after agreeing to commit this act, Mack Herring plotted and schemed on how he would do it, where he would do it, and when he would do it. Then on a bright

111

and starry night, he carried out the killing exactly as it had been planned. Did he know what he was doing? Well, the killing went exactly as planned and Betty Williams' death did not end his perfect execution of the plan. After he pulled the trigger, there was no sudden loss of consciousness and there was no collapse into remorse or hysteria. No, there was simply the execution of the plan, including an attempt to hide the body in the depths of a Winkler County stock pond. If these acts were the acts of a person dethroned of the ability to reason, shouldn't there be some evidence of a disconnect from reality, some sudden break with a pattern of behavior? But there was none. Everything went as planned and even the next day when Herring went to the pond to retrieve Betty's body, he was calm, rational, and in control. He was sane and he knew what he was doing.

Do we know why? Was there jealousy or tension between them? Mack Herring says no, but we cannot speak to Betty Williams to know her side of the case. She cannot speak, and even her letter asking us to forgive Mack of her death is silent on his motivations. Why didn't he tell anyone about her death wish? Her friends didn't take her seriously? Why did Mack take her seriously? Or did he? We don't know what he said or she said, but we do know what he did. He calmly, rationally, and efficiently carried out the plan to kill Betty Williams. Was there jealousy, or resentment, or even fear in his actions? We cannot be absolutely certain, but the defense was asked to prove by a "preponderance of the evidence" that Mack Herring did not know right from wrong when he committed this action. Note that the standard here is not whether he possibly did not know what he was doing, but that from an overwhelming body of evidence it is absolutely certain that he did not know what he was doing.

Dr. Grice has said that Mack Herring was badgered

into undertaking this killing and that he was suffering from something called "Gross Stress Disorder." Before three days ago, I had never heard of such a thing and perhaps you hadn't either, but let's take the Doctor's word for it--Gross Stress Disorder is a real thing. But does it make sense that a girl was able to generate this amount of stress in only eleven minutes of talking? Eleven minutes, sometimes with other people around. It doesn't make sense to me, and I am sure it doesn't make sense to you. The true nature of this matter needs to be determined in a trial. Justice demands that we get to the bottom of this whole event. I am certain that we have more to learn, and I will dedicate myself to uncovering even more of this mystery before that trial occurs. But, as far as these proceedings are concerned, look at the evidence. There was a plan and that plan was carried out exactly--Mack Herring's behavior was calculated, efficient and, most of all, rational. You have to find that he was sane when he killed Betty Williams. There is really no other explanation for his behavior. Thank you.

It was close to 5:00 PM on Saturday afternoon. Every ounce of emotion had been wrung from the participants and the spectators, but now it was out of the lawyers' hands. Old-timers and teenagers alike thought that both closing arguments were strong, but how the jury would rule was totally clear. Judge Olsen read them the charge and it was just as Warren Burnett said it would be. The jury had to a make a single determination: "Do you find from a preponderance of the evidence that at the time of the act charged by the indictment in this case, the defendant, John Mack Herring, was insane?"

The jury left the courtroom to initiate its deliberations at 5:07 PM.

-- Shel Hershorn

CHAPTER XX
The Verdict

The jury met late into the night on Saturday night. Eventually they sent a note out asking to see the testimony of Dr. Grice, but the clerk could not find it. Judge Olsen had no choice but to send the jury home for the rest of the weekend while they secured the transcript. By Monday morning the clerk had found the doctor's testimony, and the jury wished to hear it in its entirety. For an hour-and-a-half, the clerk read the testimony as the jury hung on his every word. They then went back to the jury room for another five hours when, at around 3:45 PM, they sent a note out saying that they were hopelessly deadlocked and could come to no conclusion. The note indicated that the vote was 10-2. Judge Olsen did not declare a mistrial. Instead he sent a note back to the jury room to tell them to continue their deliberations for a bit longer. He wanted them to do their best to come to a unanimous decision.

Just before the Judge sent the note back, Dan Sullivan filed a complex four-point motion calling for a mistrial anyway on the grounds that the Judge should never have allowed a hearing on the sanity instead of a trial for murder. Judge Olsen dismissed it, but Sullivan told the press that regardless of the outcome this case would be around for a long time to come. Eventually, after a few more hours, the jury informed the Judge that it had come to a unanimous decision. The reading of the decision, however, was further delayed when the Judge discovered that the jury had made a "technical error," the nature of which was unclear. Finally, the jury gathered back into the courtroom where the Judge looked at the jury's decision and then asked the jury foreman, Mr. Autry Reid, if in fact the jury had reached a unanimous decision. Mr. Reid assured the Judge that they had. Judge Olsen then asked the foreman to read the jury's response to the following question:

"Do you find from a preponderance of the evidence that at the time of the act charged by the indictment in this case, the defendant, John Mack Herring, was insane?"

In a firm and steady voice, Autry Reid declared: "Yes."

Warren Burnett collapsed in tears. Mrs. Herring cried and embraced her son. Mr. Herring fell to a knee in front of his family and hugged them both. Mack Herring put both hands to his face as it contorted in tears. Burnett insisted on shaking each juror's hand as he told them "thank you." Joe and Mary Belle Williams appeared stunned as onlookers rushed to the Herring family's side to offer congratulations. Eventually they worked their way to the back of the courtroom and then slipped away into the night.

Dan Sullivan again insisted that the case was far from over. He would appeal to a higher court on the grounds that Judge Olsen had erred in allowing a separate sanity hearing. Eventually the Supreme Court of the Sate of Texas agreed with the DA, and it issued a Writ of Mandamus requiring an actual trial to be held in Beaumont, Texas in November, 1962. The rumor around Kermit was that the public criticism Judge Olsen received for the outcome of the hearing and from the Supreme Court's reversal actually killed the old man. His spirit was broken and his standing in the community was harmed, but who can say why someone dies? The trial in Beaumont was anti-climatic. Though the records of the trail cannot be located, we know that the jury's decision there was essentially the same as it was in Kermit. Mack Herring was found innocent of murder on the grounds on temporary insanity. The strange case of Betty and Mack was over.

-- Shel Hershorn

CHAPTER XXI
Rabbit Huntin'

"Bill Martin is comin' down from Goreville next week, Shelly Bill. Let's take him rabbit huntin'," said my dad. He knew that I hated to hunt, but he also knew that I could find the best places to find rabbits. One absolute rite of passage for West Texas boys is jack-rabbit hunting. Jacks swarm the West Texas plains, and you can find them easily just a mile or two outside of Odessa if you know which oilfield road had the least amount of traffic. Back then I was also a good shot. As early as eleven years old, I won the American Legion "Turkey Shoot" by placing four of five shots near a bulls eye a hundred yards away. When my friends and I went hunting rabbits, I often used the twenty-two barrel of my H&R Over and Under Rifle instead of the 410 shotgun shell my friends preferred. I still bagged more jacks than my friends, but it didn't really matter. We shot the rabbits and left them on the side of the road. Mostly we told jokes, talked football, and made fun of one another. In truth we were just fulfilling whatever genetic dictate hunting requires of teenage males.

Jackrabbit killing barely merits being called hunting. It is definitely not sport. At least it isn't the way we did it. We'd drive to the edge of town before the sun came up, turn our headlights on bright, place two guys with shotguns over each headlight, and then drive slowly down some dusty road. The confused jacks would be stunned by the bright lights and would either stare at the beam transfixed or dart across the road after a momentary pause. The hesitation would usually cost them their life. Most guys would blast them with a shotgun from perhaps a twelve-foot range. Most such trips ended with the sheer boredom with killing so many rabbits. Of course, there was no "limit" on the number one could kill, but we eventually tired of it anyway.

The early December morning my dad chose to take my uncle rabbit hunting was quite chilly, perhaps in the low forties. I saw no purpose in it. My dad never went rabbit hunting with us or his friends, but he may have wanted to show my uncle that there really was something manly I could do. Neither my dad nor my uncle cared about my football games and they could care less about my baseball abilities. The odd thing about the morning was that when we got to the other side of town to my Uncle Joe's, Betty had been asked to go along with us. I could not believe my eyes, for Betty hated (is there a stronger word for hate?) all forms of hunting and killing.

"Jackrabbits are living creatures, Shell. How can you murder them?" she said, repeating a script we had played for years.

"They are scrawny, bug-infested pests," I retorted.

"Yes, living bug-infested pests. Whatever happened to the sanctity of life, Cuz?" she'd argue.

"So why don't you stay at home?" I concluded.

"Can't, Shell. Daddy says family comes first, and this is my only chance to see your Uncle Bill," she said.

That was curious to me since Uncle Bill was in fact my uncle, not hers, and the whole time we were together I never saw her talk with or interact with Uncle Bill a single time. What a strange hold Joe had over her. As it was the five of us piled into my dad's Caddy and headed for the oil patch. Betty, Uncle Bill and I were in the backseat, while my dad and Uncle Joe were in the front. Betty messed with me the whole way. She slipped her leg under mine; she complained about being cold until I put my arm around her; she whispered in my ear about how fat Uncle Bill had gotten; and she talked openly about how stupid hunting was. The men didn't seem to notice us since they were engrossed in gossiping about Southern Illinois and drinking early morning beers.

When we got to the edge of town, Daddy asked me where to find jack. I picked a road my buddies and I had used before. Upon entering the road, Daddy stopped and he and Uncle Bill positioned themselves on the headlights. Uncle Joe drove. Betty and I stayed in the backseat. As soon as we started the slow creep down the road, Betty started in on me again about the inhumanity of hunting.

"I don't see why you do it, Shell. It's not for food, and it isn't sport."

"They are pests," I said, "and it helps the ranchers."

"What ranchers, Shell, we are in the middle of oil leases as far as the eye can see," she argued.

"Oh, I don't know, Betty. Anyway, I don't much care one way or another. You know I don't really like to hunt," I responded weakly.

"So, don't do it! Don't kill anything today, Shell. For me, OK, for me?" she implored.

She had almost convinced me, but after a while, the car stopped. My dad jumped (more like fell) off the left headlight and came back to the driver's side of the car. As he opened the car, I could hear Uncle Bill laughing.

"Shelly Bill, you get out here," he said. "I can't see good enough to hit a damned thing and I'm tired of hearing this sorry, fat SOB laughing at me. But he hasn't hit anything either."

He motioned me out of the backseat, and handed me my Over and Under. I took it, reached back into the car to retrieve my Permian football jacket, and walked to the front of the car. I mounted the driver's side headlight like a cowboy slinging his leg onto his horse. That was a natural move for me, but my Uncle Bill noticed anyway.

"Impressive, Shelton," he said. "Now let's see if you are as good a shot as your Daddy says you are."

There it was. My dad wanted to show me off to this Illinois farmer. Of all the stupid things, I thought. He wants me to put on a shooting display and my cousin wants me not to kill innocent animals. At first I decided to ignore my cousin's entreaties, since the rabbits were over-abundant and the idea of my dad's being happy with me was a unique and special feeling. Unfortunately, I missed my first shot quite by accident. From deep inside the car, I heard my dad yell out "God Dammit, Shelly Bill!" Right then and there I decided that no jackrabbits were gonna die that morning. From then on I shot high and I shot low. I shot wide and I shot far. But I sure as hell didn't shoot straight. Betty later reported to me that my dad muttered obscenities almost all the rest of the way. Finally he grew silent. Outside my Uncle Bill made no comments. He could tell that his sister's son was missing on purpose and he thought it best to let it go.

I have never killed another animal since that day. It may be because Betty convinced me it was wrong to do so or it may be because four months later she was felled by a sportsman. A person with a life-long passion for killing took her life. His explanation for how easy it was to dispose of her body disabused me of hunting forever. I will never forget that putting her into and taking her out of a stock pond was like handling a "dead cat on the side of the road." I could never hunt jackrabbits again.

CHAPTER XXII
"What Do You Believe?"

Betty Williams at seventeen was a prolific writer. Her eloquent note exonerating Mack Herring made her a witness for the defense. But that note was far from the only piece of her writing that the police gathered in evidence. Some of the writings Dan Sullivan did not consider relevant for the hearing or the trial and some of it Warren Burnett successfully prevented from being entered into evidence. Perhaps the most intriguing mystery regarding her writing were two items that "various witnesses" told the police about but were never found. One was a diary and the other was a letter that she left in her home the night she went with Ike and Mack. The police came to the small house on Henderson looking for these items more than once, but Betty's mom insisted that she had checked the house thoroughly and neither item was anywhere to be found.

Still Betty had a lot to say. In one essay entitled "What Do You Believe" for her senior English class Betty concluded with these thoughts:

> Soon we will be older and grown up, really
> grown up, and we'll be made to realize and believe in
> [different] things. Perhaps before we are completely

grown, we'll be made to believe in war, hate and death just as our parents before us have learned. ...I believe in happiness, the kind of happiness after you have triumphed over pain and sorrow. I believe in the laughter that comes with [such] happiness, laughter reflecting the tears of yesterday and the hopes of tomorrow.

A tomorrow that never came.

In a note to *"Charles"*:

...I am realizing once again, as I have realized so may times before, that in some ways not completely obvious to me, I am different from other people.

Most people don't understand me. There are people who are willing to be my friends, but mostly they are too ignorant to understand why I am like I am and consequently offer my mind no challenge; or they haven't the wits to match mine...

In a random piece of writing:

I've finally become 17 years old, finally become a senior. I have so many hopes and dreams. Some of my dreams have simply floated away and out of my life; others have been burst, their iridescent loveliness shattered into a million pieces. I've had troubles, maybe a little more than the next person. Teens are all inclined to be dramatic and I was worse than most. The death of a brother hit me hard; insults and slanderous gossip ruined my reputation, insults that were unjustified, and cut so deeply there is still a scar. Things that I thought were surely mine were suddenly torn from me; friends, parents, hopes, even my belief in God. For awhile I became what many kids termed to be "a beat." I wore my long hair straight, white lipstick, gobs of eye make-up and spent hours reading Jack Kerouac. I spoke sadly of the world. It was all an act, yes, but few people saw through it, least of all, me. I was unhappy, depressed.

Finally one day a friend looked me straight in the eyes and told me what I was, not what I thought I was, a beat, a sophisticate, but what I really was, a girl for which he has no respect, a girl who was ruining her life. I began to see then what I was doing. It was then that I found God again, waiting right where I left Him. You would think everything would be all right again, wouldn't you? But it wasn't. I began to blame God if things didn't go right, ask Him for things that I had no right to ask for. Into my life came one great Want. I felt that if I couldn't have this, I couldn't go on living. It possessed my whole life. I couldn't sleep at night...

To "Will":

Will, why? Why, in the name of all of God's earth, can't we arrive at some compromise?

Though you never speak to me, seldom look at me, but often snub me yet, all the same you're pulling, tugging at my very soul until my whole being is strained and tense with the effort of controlling myself. I ask myself over and over: Why? Why must it be this way?

Yes, yes, yes, I realize now that what I did with you was wrong but must you condemn me for it? You have condemned me, you know? Maybe not with your lips but your every action cries hatred and damnation for all eternity.

And yet even with all that you're more

125

tolerant than Mack. He hates me for what I did to him, for what I made him do to himself and yet he can't express his hatred in rage. He makes sly digs causing me to writhe in embarrassment and fear. Daily he punishes me, making remarks that no one understands but me but that I feel the entire world knows what he is doing to me and is applauding him and cheering him on.

Do you hate me? Can you find it in your heart to hate someone as small and tormented as me? You have hurt me far more than I have hurt you. Your eyes, when they happen to meet mine, are filled with a strange expression, or mixed expressions, that I cannot identify. I long to talk to you but I know there is very little that we could say. Though you laugh and talk and joke with others, the thought of me causes you to hush instantly. Why? Why? What in God's name causes you to halt in your merriment? Is the memory of our time together so distasteful to you? Do you remember it with disgust?

Can't you see what you are doing to me? I go through hell every day, a hell that we created together, you and me, and now (only) I am forced to live in it.

Can you not find it in your heart to forgive me and be friendly? Yes, I am jealous. I get so jealous of you that I could scream and gnash my teeth and beat the trees in my rage. If I thought I could, perhaps, in some way bring you back to me, I would spare no effort to make you mine.

I would be better off were you dead. Then I could perhaps forget you. But now I am daily constrained to see you and not speak to you, to love you and know that I am hated.

I hate myself for loving you and yet I hang onto my love for you as though it could pull me out of this pit of darkness I am forced to inhabit.

My entire being cries Will, Will, Will. Even the birds mock me with their cries of Will, Will, Will.

And your friends! They know, don't they? Yes, yes, I am sure they do. They give me their hard, knowing glances and I must pretend not to see. Pretense! You must pretend not to know me; I must pretend not to care for you. Mack must pretend that it was his idea to break up. Steve must pretend to ignore me and dear sweet Dan and Jerry must pretend that they know nothing of the whole affair. God, my God, everything is one, huge distorted lie!

Will, can't you see what you are doing to me? You're ruining me. You've torn me to bits. Half of me cries out to you and the other half recoils in fear.

I cannot even pray any more. I know that God is so far away I cannot reach Him. All I can do is cry piteously, God, MY God, Please God, Please.

And yet He never hears me!

Mack,

Well, I guess you accomplished what you set out to do. You hurt me, more than you will ever know. When you handed me that note this morning, you virtually changed the course of my life. I don't [know] what I expected that note to say. I'll not waste time saying that I didn't deserve it because I guess I did. I have never been so hurt in my life and I guess your note was the jolt I needed to get me back on the straight and narrow. I've done a lot of things, I know, that were bad and cheap, but I swear before God that I didn't mean them to be like that; I was just showing off. I know it's much too late with you, Mack, but I swear that another boy won't get the chance to say what you said to me. You've made me realize that instead of being smart and sophisticated like I thought, I was only being cheap and ugly and whorish.

Forgive me for writing this last note and thank you for reading it. I won't trouble you again, and, Mack, I haven't forgotten the good times we had. I have really enjoyed knowing you and I'm awfully sorry it had to end this way.

I realize that this is the end of our friendship: Thanks again for straightening me out. Believe me there is not going to be any just cause for criticism for behavior on my part ever again. Sherry may know everything, but she's still willing to be my friend. She's going to help me and you don't know how much her friendship means to me. If you ever need to tell me anything, go to Annabelle.

Best of luck with your steady girlfriend. I hope she's the best.

Betty

PS When you think of me, try to think of the good times we had and not of this.

From another school essay:

Life is full of pitfalls which must be avoided if man is to arrive at the end of his journey unblemished by life's ugliness. But, falling into disrepute, one need [not] give in wholly to despair, for just as surely as there is a path into darkness, there is, too, a path out of it. Hope is the light which [illuminates] man's way out of the blackness.

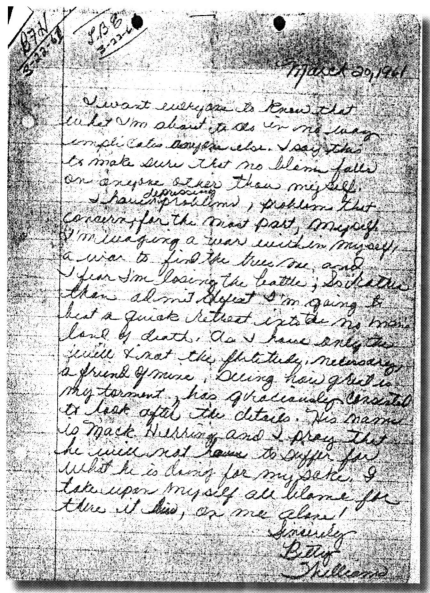

Betty's Last Composition

CHAPTER XXIII
"Little Egypt"

"It's just so wrong. He's the victim and she's the bad guy." My new girlfriend, Janell Hollis, said that to me even before she knew that Betty was my cousin. Unlike most of the other students at Permian that spring of 1962, she had paid attention to the hearing going on in Kermit. It was on the front page of the Odessa American every day, but kids don't read the newspaper. The kids at OHS involved in the hearing were engaged in it, but most of the rest of them and almost all of us had more important things on our minds than a year-old murder case. A friend of mine wondered why I was "obsessed" with the case. I was and Janell was, too. To us the events in Kermit challenged what we thought we knew about the difference between right and wrong, good and evil. OK, perhaps all teenagers are dramatic, but there it was. To many who did pay attention to the trial and to the gossip surrounding the trial, Betty deserved to die because she was a "bad person," and she had led Mack astray. It was just so wrong.

What got to me then and what gets to me now is that no one ever even tried to figure out what lay behind Betty's "problems and stresses." That was not part of the hearing and it certainly wasn't part of the investigation. She was depicted as a strange and disturbed

131

girl. To many of the kids at OHS she was a slut and an outcast. Worse, she was a diabolical manipulator who could influence a strong and confident football player into killing her. Friends of mine on the west side of town and in Kermit heard it often, once even from one of the jurors over the weekend break in the hearing, "That Betty Williams was 'nothin'. She wasn't worth anything." No single event in my life ever had the impact on me that Betty's death and trial had. I was radicalized. Parental authority, women as sexual objects, marriage, athletes' place in society, and most of all the justice system in America all looked different to me from then on. Of course, time, world events, and getting older modified my views over the coming decades, but for me the '60s really started in 1961. For a long while Betty was my mentor in approaching life. I would forever celebrate the counter culture and the absolute need for there to be a counter culture.

But I would never be part of it. Life's twists and turns and perhaps the fear of making some of Betty's mistakes pulled me back. Take, for example, the events following the days and weeks after the hearing. I was furious and depressed that no one had stood up for Betty or Betty's reputation. I wanted to confront my aunt and uncle; I wanted to find Will Rosebud and call him out as a liar; I wanted to tell Dan Sullivan that he had known Betty so little that he didn't realize that there was real probability that Betty never wanted to die. My guess was that she had told Mack that she was pregnant with his child. That he had to marry her to get her away from her parents and Odessa itself. No, she wasn't pregnant, but she was willing to do or say anything to win him back and get away. What was she doing out there? Trying to win him back for the long run or have sex with him just one more time. What was he afraid of? Being trapped with this loser? His parents' reaction if he really had knocked her up? More emotional confrontations? Why didn't anyone even think to explore these possibilities? Because they could not imagine that kids would operate at that level of manipulation or fear? Were her problems and stresses so inconsequential that no one even wanted to discover what they were or how her behavior fell into a pattern? I wanted to "rage against the machine" in those first few weeks after the hearing, but I never did. I became too busy trying to prevent my own father from having Mack Herring killed.

One day abut a week after the hearing I went to work at my dad's car wash. He had never said a word about the hearing, not one word. In our family from that day forward we never talked about it again. But my buddy Gro took me aside one more time to warn me that something was up. Kingfish was acting funny and he had been on the phone a couple of times talking in conspiratorial tones. Gro, who knew where every peephole and crack was in that old car wash, naturally took up a spot where he could hear Daddy talk. What he heard was a discussion about "taking out that little son-of-a bitch." Gro had no doubt that he was talking about Mack Herring, and I had no doubt to whom Daddy was speaking. It had to be Earl Shelton or one of his "associates."

Daddy's family was from Southern Illinois. It just so happened that for the greater part of the Twentieth Century most of Southern Illinois was the home turf of one of the country's most notorious gangs, the biggest concentration of organized crime outside of Chicago as matter of fact. There were several gangs and several legendary gangsters in "Little Egypt," but the most feared bunch of them all was the "Notorious Shelton Brothers." Various books have cataloged their exploits, but we didn't know them from history books. They were part of our lives. Once in 1945 just after Daddy got out of the service, he stopped by a roadside tavern to have a morning drink. It was around 10:30 AM. Daddy was at one end of the bar and some other guy was at the other end. With the bartender, only three people were in the place. Suddenly one of the Shelton Gang walked into the bar, pumped four or five bullets into the other fellow at the bar and then looked straight at Daddy: "You see anything, Kink?" Daddy shook his head no. The guy nodded at the bartender, turned, and walked out.

OK, my name is Shelton, but my parents say that it is just

a coincidence that one of the men my dad respected most, Dr. John Shelton, a vet, just happened to share the last name of a gangster. Still, Daddy knew those guys and when he faced an insoluble problem like Mack Herring, he thought about finding out what it would cost to "take out" Mack. When Gro told me about the conversation he had overheard, I knew exactly to whom Daddy was talking and what he wanted. I dreaded confronting him about it because he rarely changed his mind when it was made up. Besides, he was already furious at me for telling him that I was going to go to the University of Texas to study Political Science, called Government at UT. He wanted me to stay in town, go to Junior College, and enroll in Car Wash Management School. We would eventually nearly come to blows on this whole "stay in West Texas" issue, but first I had to convince him not to commission a murder.

Janell was incredulous when she heard all this. "What is wrong with you people?" I really had no good answer to that particular question, though she would ask it many times over the ensuing few weeks and then over the next forty years. But in 1962 her advice was the same as it would always be in these circumstances: "You have to confront your dad on this. He can't be allowed to commit murder." What? No more pretending? No more ignoring reality? Talk to your father. I admit that I eventually got the courage to do it not just because my girlfriend told me to do so. I decided that I had to do it because Betty had not talked to her father. I wasn't sure why she hadn't, but I knew that he was a big part of her problems, a huge part of her stresses. How bad had it been? What parts did I not know? No, I had to talk to mine or else I would be morally responsible for the taking of another person's life.

"It's a tempting offer," Daddy said. He readily admitted talking to the Shelton Brothers not once but two or three times. Everyone in Southern Illinois was aware of the events in West Texas. They knew about Betty, about Mack, and about the verdict. They were outraged. The gangsters in Little Egypt thought there had been a grave miscarriage of justice in West Texas. How could a guy kill a poor girl like that and never go to jail or even have to get psychological counseling? They told Daddy that he would kill Mack Herring personally - for free - if Daddy would just say the word. "How about that lawyer, too?" he was asked. All Daddy had to do was give them the word. I didn't have to talk Daddy out of it. He had decided not to take them up on the offer. The Odessa Sheriff, Slim Gabrel, already had his eye on my dad, it seems. During the hearing, he personally came to my dad's car wash and confiscated Daddy's Colt .45 pistol. When Daddy asked him why, Slim just said they wanted to be sure that he "behaved." Smart as Slim was, he probably would have figured out who was behind a gangland killing of Mack Herring, Daddy said. Playing tough guy, I said "Well, that's true, but you could always hire Warren Burnett."

"Not in this lifetime," Daddy said, "Not in this lifetime."

Bill (Kink) Williams (right) Stylin' in Little Egypt

Chapter XXIV
The Ghost of Odessa High

"Who was Betty Williams?" I asked. A chorus of voices responded.

"The Original Drama Mama!"

"The Ghost of OHS!"

"The girl who asked a football player to shoot her!"

I was sitting in Nancy Shacklett's den two hours after Permian had defeated OHS in football for the twenty-first straight year. Nancy, who went to Permian with me in the early sixties, now had a daughter, Shanna, who attended OHS. The students gathered there were her friends and the '80s version of who Nancy and I had been two decades earlier. The loss to Permian had not been easy for them to digest, for they had predicted to me before the game that this would be "the year" that the Permian jinx would be broken. They would have to wait for not only another year but almost another century for that to happen.

Nevertheless, they were in high spirits and quite willing to talk to this old guy who was asking about Betty Williams. Nancy had just introduced me as a "friend she had gone to high school with." I was with another man, Mark David, whom I hoped would help me write a book about my cousin. As Mark and I sat there for over an hour, the kids told us the story. They knew it quite well, even though they exaggerated how beautiful she was and how great a football player Mack was.

What impressed us most was their interpretation of Betty's significance to their lives. "She was the patron saint of weird kids," one girl concluded. Her comment was a compliment, not a put down, and the other kids agreed. "Sure," one guy said, "she's always there for all the band geeks, hippies, and theater types."

"She's where?" I asked.

"Don't you know?" came the choral response amid the giggles.

I did, but I wanted to hear them say it, so I said: "No, tell me."

"She haunts the OHS Theater. To see her all's you have to do is go to the parking lot across from the Theater at midnight. At the exact stroke of twelve, honk your horn three times and say her name, Betty! She'll come right to the Theater window. She's so cool!" The girl telling the story was the one who had spoken up earlier. She seemed to care more about Betty than the football game, and that was a real shock to me. In truth they all seemed to care more about Betty. She was important to them.

It was already 11:30 PM, so the natural thing to do was to go over to OHS. The kids suggested it, but if they had not, Mark and I were prepared to do so. OHS was less than a mile away, but I had not seen it in twenty-six years. We all piled into our cars and for a brief moment I was a teenager running the streets of Odessa again. Car radios were automatically turned to the Oldies station and the Big Bopper's Chantilly Lace filled the air. I expected only to be an observer on the trip, but when we pulled into the parking lot at OHS, I was overwhelmed. The red bronco on the side of the building always thrilled me. The Theater itself, jutting out from the middle of the building, always struck me as a special place. Memories of *Puss and Boots* and *Alice in Wonderland* reminded me that I had come here as a child long before Betty had performed on its stage. From the field house on the south side of the building to the administrative offices on the north, OHS was my school, too. Proms, basketball games, and Student Council exchanges had brought me here. Betty brought me back and, according to legend, she was still here. Was she waiting for me? Was she up there hoping to say good-bye to me?

No, I don't believe in ghosts, but in researching this book a few odd things had happened. Mark had arranged for us to meet with a Psychic who seemed to know or guess the main outline of Betty's story. She also said that Betty "desperately" wished to contact me to "ease my mind." A Dallas hand-writing expert had told Mark and me that the famous note Warren Burnett had introduced at the hearing was in fact "dictated" and not a "free-flowing composition." A PhD in Psychology had listened carefully to the story and opined that Betty's behavior was surely the product of abuse, but another person who actually knew Betty argued that Betty, except for that last week, was the "coolest, most together" person she knew in high school. If ghosts arise from the deaths of people with unresolved issues, with messages to deliver, was my coming to OHS Betty's last chance?

At midnight we honked our horns and whispered her name. Only then as I looked skyward to the Theater's windows on the second story of the building did I notice that they had been painted over. She could not appear in them; they had been blacked out. We all sat there a few minutes. Roy Orbison's *Only the Lonely* played on the radio. The kids chattered away while Mark and I sat in silence. Eventually the high schoolers had to move on. A car pulled up beside us and the true believer girl rolled down her window to deliver me a message: "we missed the exact stroke of midnight. She can't come unless it's exact. Nice to meet ya!" They drove away.

Mark and I did not leave. Each of us nursed a beer. I never thought we'd see a ghost, but then a funny feeling hit me. Perhaps I needed to go up the steps to the door and give it a pull. Maybe she waited there on the other side to say good-bye or to tell me she forgave me or perhaps to reveal a secret. I got out of the car and walked across the lot. I proceeded up the steps to the well-lit door.

The darkness from the other side of the door didn't seem frightening or menacing. Was it welcoming? I reached for the door and pulled it with both hands. Nothing. It was locked tight. That is when I felt scared and wondered why in the hell I was roaming around a high school past midnight.

I virtually ran back to the car. Mark had tracked my every move. We had not spoken for nearly an hour, but all he said when I slid back into the car seat was: "Think you should have tried another door?

"No," I said. "There's no use."

We sat there for maybe ten minutes more. Suddenly someone rapped three times on the car window. Mark and I jumped, looked at each other, and then saw the Odessa policeman motioning for me to get out of the car. I came out talking. I am not as imaginative as my dad, but I talked fast. Essentially I told him the whole story of Mack and Betty, Betty's ghost, and my book in two minutes.

"Oh, yes," he said. "We know the story, Mr. Williams. Everyone out here knows the story. That's why the windows were painted and sealed shut. Too many kids came out here too many nights. I assumed that's what you were doing, but I had to make sure you weren't vandals. You know, the game tonight might bring them out."

"Yes, sir," I said. "We are just leaving."

Driving away from OHS left me feeling empty, but I was smiling.

"Well, you got what you came for," Mark said.

"Yes, I did," I said. We both knew that I had not come for ghosts or scary stories. I had not come for high school nostalgia or a football game. I had not come to wallow in the past. No, I had come to see if Betty's life had a legacy, and indeed it had. Betty was the Original Drama Mama, the "Patron Saint of Weirdoes."

I was so proud.

CHAPTER XXV
The Reunion

"Sure, that girl wanted to die. She asked me to kill her too." Martin Rodriquez had gained forty pounds and lost most of his hair since his high school days. At the hearing in 1962, he said the same thing. Now we were standing in the atrium of the Holiday Inn half way between Odessa and Midland. The 1962 graduating classes of OHS and Permian were jointly celebrating their twenty-fifth reunions. The rumor was that Tommy Lombardo himself would be at the reunion. "Cruisin' Tommy's" stories could be heard everywhere. A large number of people came up to Janell and me to talk about Betty. Some asked us what we knew about Mack, Warren Burnett, Betty's folks, but most just wanted to talk about the incident. A lot of the girls/women from both schools ardently insisted that Betty had never intended to die. She was acting out, making a plea for help or attention, or just engaging in some kinky role-playing before sex.

"What does a 'Drama Mama' wear to her own death?" asked Pam Wilhelm, Permian. "She'd dress in all black or all white. Something flowing. Not sexy, shorty pajamas!" Some argued that Betty was simply before her time. Others, who had trained in Psychology, speculated that her pattern of promiscuity suggested, sorry, Shell, sexual abuse, probably by her father. The men, for the most part, believed none of this. The girl wanted to die. There was plenty of evidence to suggest that, and besides why not take her at her word? She told maybe six boys she wanted it. Ok, maybe, they were all Mack's friends and she knew the word would get back to him, but she meant it. She was messed up.

One morning at the motel coffee shop an OHS grad, Mike Moses, asked me if I really wanted to know what had happened. He knew. He had a wild and flawed story. Mack had not acted alone. A close mutual friend of ours, an OHS grad of diminished mental capacity, was with Mack when he killed her. Hiring Burnett, rallying the OHS kids, attacking Betty's character, all that was designed to protect someone else. His parents didn't believe their son and they didn't especially like each other. He heard that they divorced soon after the trial. (I knew that wasn't true.) Mack's parents, Mike said, paid Burnett the big bucks to protect the other kid, who was more like a son to them than Mack was. He went on. Mike, I said, I don't want to hear it. I long ago let go of any resentment of Mack or his parents. Even Warren Burnett doesn't interest me any more. That is an incredible story. It might even be true, but I have no interest in pursuing such a theory or such speculation any more. Let them all rest or rest in peace.

I was only partially lying. I never wanted to hear the bizarre theories about Mack's family, even back then. Mack's state of mind had once concerned me a great deal, but after twenty years or so, I let it go. On the other hand, Betty's motivations, Betty's behavior, and her reputation always intrigued me. Obsessed me? No, I went to the University of Texas, on to graduate school, and then began a career as a college professor. No, I didn't teach Psychology or Gender Studies or Criminal Justice. I taught International Relations --something about as far from West Texas as it could be. That matched my desire to leave West Texas forever. Except to visit Janell's family or, on rare occasion, to tour the old haunts of Odessa, I had left it behind. My gang of guys, her posse of girls, old teachers, anyone and anything were left behind. But what Betty was up to those three days in March 1961 never really left my mind. Thanksgiving and Christmas, when certain songs played on the radio, and even the look of certain women I passed on the streets of New York, Washington, or Dallas reminded me of her and the events of 1961.

How could it be otherwise? Men and women approached me privately at the reunion to tell me that Betty's death or Betty or the trial affected the course of their lives. Most felt a sense of guilt for "not having done something." Some were tortured by how her character was assassinated at the trial. They became ardent feminists. One had been one of "Mack's girls" at the trial. Afterwards she quit as cheerleader and began, without shame, to pursue singing, and not just singing, but opera. She could care less if Odessa boys mocked opera or disliked intellectuals. She was going to be herself. Betty was the first "Hippy," she said. She was her role model for the rest of the sixties.

The reunion was fun. Tommy showed up. People told funny stories about Tommy's, about football games, and about how silly we all were. Janell and I visited lost and forgotten friends and we swapped stories as well. At the closing dance, we jitter-bugged. Who knew Shell could dance? Still I watched the door. Would Mack come? This was his reunion too. He lived in Odessa. He knew everyone there. He didn't show. But as I stood there looking at all those middle-aged folks, it all came back again. I was transported back to that time and place. It hit me especially hard when one guy walked in. He had an open collar shirt and he was wearing a gold medallion. His tanned body was slim and firm. He worked at a yachting club in California. His wife was twenty years younger, and my buddy Steve told me that he was pretty sure they had been snorting coke in the bathroom. His name escaped me momentarily, but what Betty had said about him had never left me. "Hey, Shell, guess who I fucked tonight?"

143

CHAPTER XXVI
Betty Jean

Betty's gift to me was to force me to think for myself. She was seventeen and I was sixteen when she died. Both of us were literally children at the time, but, of course, we didn't think of ourselves that way. I often wonder how she would have reacted to the social forces that the second half of the sixties unleashed. Would she have actually been a Hippy? Would she have become a feminist? Would she have found Jesus and reverted to her Hard Shell life? The answer is probably a combination of all of the above. She would have continued her search, however, through the arts. She would have been on the stage, behind the stage, or around the stage somewhere. She would have matured in her views and she would have gained perspective on her problems in light of the plight of others. No doubt she would have continued to be dramatic in her daily life, but the hills and valleys of her emotions would surely flattened out somewhat. I have no doubt that she would have been a hell of a woman.

For me Betty's life, and particularly her excesses, offered a cautionary note. Don't go too far. Be careful what you ask for. On the other hand, she was not just a depressed teen with both real and imaginary problems. She was a feeling, thinking human being who worried every day of her life about what is normal? Where is God? In one of her many essays, she wrote about the "rights" we have as humans and the foremost of these was the "right to feel." She did and she also communicated what she felt. Most of the kids around her, her parents, and many of the adults in Odessa just didn't want to know what she thought, experienced, or had to say. That's mostly because at that point in her life, she was experiencing and talking about relationships and about sex. She felt intensely about those issues, and they became a central focus of this society in the '60s and the '70s. Her openness, her behavior, and her love of life became the standard for the sexual revolution of the era. She was a girl though in West Texas in the early sixties. Betty had love affairs, but they had to be with someone. There were boys/men who loved her and who made love to her. No one should ever forget that her sins, her misbehavior, her indiscretions had to occur with other people who were just as guilty or just as innocent as she was. I am sure all that was a phase in her life, but as a budding young woman she embraced personal freedom and paid the price of that freedom as much as anyone I know.

The question I had when I started working on a book about Betty, the trial, and our lives in Odessa was whether or not Betty needed to die. To what degree did she actually want to die? To what degree did Mack want her to die? To what degree did he actually lose his ability to think rationally when he killed her? I still don't know. I started researching and writing this book in the early eighties. At first I thought I needed a professional writer to tell the story (and maybe I did), but the very fine person who tried for a number of years could not do it. He tried to fictionalize the book from Mack's perspective and then from Betty's. He and I interviewed witnesses at the trial, Sheriff Eddins, jurors, the drama teacher at OHS, some of Mack's girls, and others from Odessa and Kermit. Dan Sullivan would talk to us and Warren Burnett would not. Dan Sullivan told us that Warren had said that Mack was temporarily insane when he killed Betty and that he was not a danger to society. "I guess Warren was right," Mr. Sullivan concluded. After all of these interviews and perspectives, two things were clear. The Betty Williams/Mack Herring story was one of the biggest, if not the biggest, event in most of these folks' lives. And that's the second clear point. It was a big part of my life, too, and I had to write the story myself. It is partially my story, and I had to tell it -- as well or as poorly as I could.

There are so many things more important than the story of Mack and Betty: war, the economy, our jobs, the environment, our kids, our health, and, to a vast majority of Americans, their relationship to religion. But relationships and sex are part of life and communication about them both is one of life's most difficult undertakings. Teenagers are even more exposed to a sexual environment today, and they even more need to talk to someone about these things. Betty and I could communicate. She made that happen. I took her approach and her attitudes as my standard. Be open. Expect people to like sex and do it. Expect people to understand human weakness as part of being human. Try to be honest with yourself and others. But then she did not communicate with me at the end. She did not tell me if she were being sexually abused. She did not tell me that she was asking people to kill her. She did not reveal to me all of her stresses and problems. How truly open was our relationship? Was she the sophisticated and worldly person she thought she was or was she a common tramp? Or just a troubled teen? Are my own attitudes open, honest or naive? It's the human condition to worry about such things, but Betty taught me to ask questions out loud.

I will go to my grave uncertain about the answers to these questions, but I know a couple of things. Betty did not deserve to die or to be condemned for her behavior. She may have been ahead of her time or she may have been disturbed and troubled, but she was a good person. Having sex with several boys did not make her any less good. Being open and honest about it made her a social pariah. I am not sure we have not come much further since 1961, but I will speak up for Betty. She was a brilliant butterfly who was consumed by the flames, but, by God, she once lived in West Texas.

CHAPTER XXVII
Dear Betty

Dear Betty,

I miss our talks in the old Oldsmobile. Many times over the years I have wanted to see you, talk to you about the things going on in my life. Mostly I have wanted to share the joy of life after Odessa. I know, I know, it's not Odessa that made us unhappy. It was "Life with Daddy." Both of our dads are dead now. Yours died in the '80s, but in truth after you died I did not keep in touch with your family. Janell and I went over to your house in 1965 for Thanksgiving and I can't tell you how bad it was. Uncle Joe said the prayer and he went on for it seemed like twenty minutes about you, your death, and how you were now with Jesus. It was the same old shit that he pulls on every occasion. I got tired of it, and I just never went back. Someone told me that your parents went out on every date with your two sisters, Tricia and Kathy, went on in High School. I hope that isn't true, but I haven't talked with either one of them in forty

149

years. I saw Joe Wayne in Houston when my dad was there for cancer treatments in the '80s and he said we should get together to talk about "the crazy Williams" boys someday. I couldn't bring myself to do it. Joe seemed like a well put together guy, and I have always hoped that he was young enough when Uncle Joe died not to have been influenced by him. Your mom is still alive, as far as I know.

My parents are both dead. Things came to a head for Daddy and me shortly after you died. I was determined to leave Odessa and to go to UT. When it came right down to it, Daddy kicked me out of the house and refused to pay for my college education. UT was only $25 a semester when I started, but finding the housing and food money were a little hard. The summer after my freshman year, Janell and I had six jobs between us. Oh, you never met Janell. She and I started dating the year after you died. Believe it or not, we got married when I was nineteen and she was eighteen. This summer, 2007, will be our 43rd anniversary. It hasn't always been an easy road. Both of our fathers were alcoholics and we went through the '60s and '70s wondering about the things going on around us. What made it work for us is that Janell is a different kind of woman than our mothers were. From the beginning she let me know how I needed to act as part of a "couple." When I was childish, selfish, shortsighted, or bone dumb, she told me. When we had kids, she especially made me aware that how I behaved affected their emotional well-being and sense of self. Oh, she's no saint, don't get me wrong. But I think you'd love her and you'd be proud that she and I have a partnership of equals unlike what we saw in our households *growing up. We have two kids, a boy and a girl, and now we have two beautiful grand children with a third on the way.*

Daddy married Dallas. The summer Janell and I got married was a wild one. On the night Janell and I married, a drunk driver ran a stop sign as we were passing through Midland. We crashed into him and both of us slammed against the front windshield. While we weren't terribly hurt, we ended up spending our wedding night in the bed I used to sleep in as a kid! We both lost the jobs we had arranged for in Austin because as dumb kids we didn't have the phone numbers of our new employers and we didn't call to say we wouldn't be there the following Monday morning. Eventually Janell got a job with an Austin lawyer as a typist and guess what? He had just bought a car wash and his wife was managing it. So I went out there and told her I'd manage the place for her at $1.00 an hour. They appreciated the help, but it was a bad decision. Daddy found out, of course, that I was working on a rack. He and Dee came to Austin and bought the damned place. Just like that. Then after he bought it, he came back to our tiny efficiency and called my mom to tell her that there was a housing shortage in Austin and it was going to be necessary that he and Dee get a house together. Mama called back in two minutes and told him that she'd give him the divorce he had been asking for.

The long and the short of it is that I ended up working for my dad at a car wash again. He made Dee the manager and demoted me. Meanwhile he told my mom that he was going to Austin to "win me back from her." That didn't go too well. After a few weeks, I resigned the car wash and took a job at the State Health Department Bureau of Vital Statistics. I worked there the final two years of college and then Janell and I moved to Washington, DC for me to go to grad school on full scholarship. Dee and Daddy stayed married until 1977. She finally left him because of his drinking, but in truth they were really in love and it's sad they broke up. It was also hard on Janell and me. By the time they broke up, we were back in Texas. Daddy was a wreck by then. His drinking and his smoking had ruined his health. At 62 he was finished. On a visit to Odessa, he stopped his rental car right out in the middle of the Andrews Highway next to the Ector County Coliseum. He walked over to the side of the road and sat on the curb. An eighteen-wheeler smashed into his car. Over the next ten years, Daddy was either in a VA hospital or a nursing home close to us. Yes, I took care of him for the last ten years of his life. He never quit smoking, even after they took out his larynx. No, he never told me he loved me, but he obviously loved my children. As he lay shaking on his deathbed, I did tell him I loved him. By then I had also forgiven him.

My mom had a rough time of it. It might not surprise you too much that the congregation of the Second Baptist Church where she worshipped and taught Sunday school all those years shunned her after she got divorced. She never attended another church in her life and neither have I. From your funeral on I came to think of churches as social institutions that served to preserve the social values of the core membership of the church and not a place to commune with God. I went to the University Baptist

Church in Austin for a while but after Mama was shunned I never joined another church. There's more to it than that and I may reconsider later, but there it is. God and I have a personal relationship now, and I am comfortable with my decision. Mama never made a go of it on her own. She had a series of jobs, the most interesting of which was as a housemother at a girl's reform school in Crockett, Texas, but eventually she moved back to Southern Illinois to live with her sister and mother. When her mother died, she moved in with Janell and me. Come to think of it, Janell may actually be a saint for having put up with my mother for the next fifteen years. My mother not only didn't work after she moved in with us, she put down her car keys as she came in the back door and declared that she would never drive again. She didn't.

Mama died in 2003. She was 87. I am sorry I don't know much about your family. It is my fault. I know your mom didn't want a book like this written, and I am sure she won't read it. I have just gotten the impression that the tragedy of your death separated us forever. I do now believe that our mothers bore considerable responsibility for what our fathers got away with as we were growing up. I know the times were different and the man was "King of his Domain," but that whole feminine "suffering in silence" routine was destructive. I am sorry. I know you idealized both your mom and mine. From seeing how Janell was a mom and knowing what a family can actually be, I have strong views on this subject. We can still love our mothers and ourselves as flawed people, but let's be honest. They let those two men tyrannize us as kids.

I am sure you want to know about Mack and

all your friends. I have to tell you that for a while Mack was something of a celebrity in West Texas. A friend of mine went to Texas Tech and swears that he was introduced in an English class as the "famous Mack Herring." I doubt it. Now he is living in Odessa working as an electrician. I have no idea what his life is like. I don't care actually, though I know you do. I wish him no ill. While he never went to prison, I am certain that he suffered from your death and the consequences of his actions over forty years ago. You would want him forgiven and thus I do forgive him. I wish him peace of mind forever—if it were only mine to give.

You never knew the other players in your drama, Warren Burnett, Dan Sullivan, Judge Olsen, or the jurors. Warren Burnett became famous after he defended Mack. Life magazine picked him as one of America's top one hundred young men the year after the trial. He went on to become an advocate for civil and human rights in West Texas. Later he was picked as one of the top one hundred trial lawyers in Texas during the Twentieth Century. Famous lawyers like Percy Foreman and Racehorse Haynes considered him their mentor. He was a womanizing drunk with a flair for law to me, but I hear that later in his life he settled down somewhat. He died in 2002.

Olsen died soon after the hearing. Sullivan went on to serve as DA in Winkler County. I know very little about him. We interviewed Miss Woodward, your last theater teacher. She still doesn't like you much. To tell the truth I didn't like her much either and I can't understand doing "Winterset" for high school kids. Well, she was young and inexperienced when she did, but thirty years later she was still saying that Mack was a "brilliant" boy and you didn't amount to much. Oh well, to each her own. I cannot update you on people like Will Rosebud, Carol McCutcheon, Howard Sellars, or others. I have not kept up with them, though I did see some of them briefly at the 25th Reunion. They were not among the folks who wanted to talk about the events of 1961-62. We did talk to Ike Nail at length though. He has felt guilty all these years since he was with you just as Mack came to pick you up to take you to the stock pond. He thinks he could have saved your life. I told him to let it go. He had no idea what would happen and he should not feel guilty that he was preoccupied with getting laid that night. He was just seventeen, for God's sake. Besides, of all people, you'd understand.

I do miss talking with you. I had no brothers or sisters, but you were as close to me as any sister could have been. We may have drifted apart after we graduated high school, but I know the bond between us would have remained strong. Janell has been awfully tolerant of my telling your story to so many people. You had a huge impact on her as you did on so many other people. I doubt that you ever thought you'd have such an effect on people, but you did. Now, perhaps, you'll even have more. I know you'd want me to tell other teenaged girls not to be so hard on themselves. No one is, or can be, perfect. Talk to your parents. Love and respect yourself. Everyone has problems but time smoothes things out. Am I sounding like you or me now? You "beat a retreat to the no-man's land of death." I am sure that you'd say not to go there or even think of going there. That's where my guilt lies. At the end I did not, could not,

155

say those things to you. For all our talking, you did not tell me of your stresses and problems at the end. You did not tell me that you really wanted to die. I hope I did not fail you that grievously. I hope that you can forgive me if I did.

Love you always and Rest in peace,

Shell

Chapter XXVIII
So, do we look like we care about football?

On October 10, 2003, before the sun came up, a colleague and I were standing in the Odessa High School parking lot across the street from the OHS Theater. I was concerned because the darkening sky threatened to prevent our taking any good pictures of the school at daybreak. I also feared that those rain clouds might be a sign that this whole trip had been a bad idea. Ken Brodnax of the Odessa American and I had picked the date to coincide with the annual Permian-OHS football game, and I was on a one-day fall break from Austin College. He thought one more chapter on my "final thoughts" about Odessa might be an interesting read, but the beginning of my short visit has not been auspicious. My initial drive around the town the night before confirmed that Tommy's was gone, converted into a record store/head shop. The houses that Betty and I had lived in, all four of them, were still there and were even more run down, but none looked remotely like they had fifteen years ago, much less forty. Certain folks I wanted to meet or talk to were either unwilling or unable to see me. Now this, impending rain preceded by billowing cumulous West Texas nasty black clouds, put in jeopardy my goal of at least getting a few pictures of the school.

I had another concern. What if what I had written about the "Ghost of Odessa High" was no longer true? It was based on a 1986 visit to Odessa. This book is a memoir of childhood recollections and repeated tales. I really didn't want to do more research or gather more impressions. What if the current reality is far from my set of strong memories? My plan for that day was simply to gather photographic images to complement the written text of the book. Dan Setterberg, an old friend and colleague from Austin College, was going to do the honors. Dan grew up in Minnesota, but he had long been fascinated with West Texas and he had spent the first part of 2003 on his sabbatical leave taking pictures of what he called "deep West Texas." I had not seen those images yet, but I knew his work and I wanted him to take pictures for *Washed in the Blood*. With this weather, with this light, what could we really shoot? Should I chance talking to anyone simply to find that my musings were wrong or exaggerated? Brodnax wanted me to write about Odessa, but my book is about a girl and a boy in Odessa. What was there left to say?

At 7:00 AM, nearly an hour before sun up, another car drove up in the OHS parking lot about a hundred feet from us. Two girls got out and began to gather things from the car. A steady mist came down and at first they didn't see me coming. I didn't want to scare them so I called out:

"Good morning."

"Hi," one said tentatively.

"I don't mean to bother you, but I am writing a book about OHS," I said as cheerily as I could.

"Oh, cool," she said. "What about?"

"The ghost of the OHS Theater. Know about it?" I said matter-of-factly.

"No," she said, as my heart stopped and my life, minus any ghost stories, flashed before my eyes.

"It's in the field house," she said.

"What is? The ghost?" I asked. She nodded yes.

"What her name?"

"Ghost Betty," she said.

Betty's still there. Boy, is she still there.

Dan and I decided to come back later to take pictures *inside* the field house, so our time in Odessa would be well spent. Driving away from OHS that morning, I noticed for the first time the city around me. Like every American city, Odessa has the occasional new mall or store, but it looks and feels the same as it did in the sixties. Surely there are zoning laws in Odessa but whole sections of town seem simply to be temporary structures that were haphazardly constructed, abandoned, and then reused for completely different purposes ten years later. In some neighborhoods one finds "nice" houses next to dilapidated houses next to mobile homes--wood next to vinyl next to brick next to asphalt shingles. There are plenty of pretty houses and nice neighborhoods and the small downtown is no better and no worse than the average small city, but the absolute randomness of the place is striking. I will also put Odessa up against any town in America for tacky points of entry. You can approach the place from north, east, south or west and be guaranteed to find "independently run" cheap motels, beer joints, the occasional titty bar, junked up auto repair shops, oilfield equipment grave yards, and garish, amateurishly-drawn commercial signs on every single one of them. Two blocks later you'll find a Baptist church or a Church of Christ as well. Odessans are still obviously determined not to be, or even to look like, those orderly, neat, prim and proper snooty bastards over in Midland. Tall City indeed.

Naturally what mattered in Odessa this particular Friday was the upcoming football game. Evidence of the impending match was everywhere. The newspaper recounted the history of the rivalry and the futility of the OHS cause. The school had won only four, tied one and lost thirty-eight since the beginning of the series in 1959. Cars around town proudly displayed school colors and support messages. Naturally the football fever was most prominent at the two schools—

OHS and Permian. Banners, streamers, and signs festooned both high schools and everyone in each school was decked out in their respective colors. Teachers and staff at OHS wore red shirts and blouses while the teachers and staff at Permian wore black. After several down seasons the signs at Permian conveyed the essential theme that "Mojo is back" while at OHS the signs announced "No mo' Mojo" and "Here Kitty Kitty." This was certainly the city H. G. Bissinger describes in *Friday Night Lights.*

That book! Odessans claim to hate it. Bissinger, a Philadelphia reporter, came to Odessa in 1987, lived among Odessans, and gained access to the Permian football program. He then wrote a New York Times best seller about the team and the town that loves it. Unfortunately, he also wrote about racism, anti-intellectualism and fanaticism in Odessa. People from Odessa felt betrayed since they expected a paean to the mighty Mojo football dynasty, not a dramatic rendering of the excesses and foibles of overly zealous fans who want to win at all costs. People from Midland chortled and once again felt superior. *Sixty Minutes* did a story and then repeated it about how angry Odessans were at Bissinger and how dangerous it was for him to return there for a book signing. What a lot of folks in West Texas missed in *Friday Night Lights,* however, was Bissinger's insistence that his story of misplaced priorities and shallow values was not intended to be limited to Permian, to Odessa, to West Texas, or to even Texas. Odessa was just the perfect vehicle for his social critique because Permian is so good at high school football and its fans are so loyal. Moreover, whatever is good or bad about America seems to be even more so in Odessa. Odessans live large.

I have to admit, however, that I wanted to avoid any discussion of *Friday Night Lights* in this book. While it looms large in my description of the importance of football in Odessa and in various other aspects of my story, I am not an outsider writing about Odessa. I am from there. Friends and even family have made me promise not to "do a hatchet job" on Odessa like Bissinger did. There was no use in arguing whether or not *Friday Night Lights* was a hatchet job and there was no use in my telling them that I briefly befriended Bissinger in the '90s and he truly loves some of the people about whom he wrote. I figured that *Friday Night Lights* was a relic of the late '80s and aside from an occasional question here and there, it would not be relevant to my book. I was wrong. One of the first things Dan and I heard driving around Odessa was that *Friday Night Lights* was being done as a movie and Universal Studios was going to do it. Later that evening at the OHS-Permian game the Studio executives making the movie were seated behind the Permian band in Section C of the stadium and their movie cameras roamed the sidelines. When the execs were introduced, Permian fans applauded. Is all forgiven? Do they assume the movie's themes will be different from the book's? What's going on here?

My view is that the *Friday Night Lights* book missed a lot of the great aspects of Odessa and its people not because Bissinger wasn't aware of the colorful characters, the symphony, the Globe Theater, and the many other attributes of the bands, theater programs, and all the rest of the wonderful activities the schools offer, but because Odessans themselves did not celebrate them or, crassly, did not market them as they did the black magic of Mojo football. That is no longer the case as sign after sign on US 20 announces that you are approaching Odessa, Texas, the "Land of Contrasts." The symphony, the Globe Theater, the educational institutions, and much more are now so much more part of the informational landscape. Perhaps Odessa has actually benefited form the outsider's critique, but don't say that too loudly in West Texas.

How much has it changed for the high school kids? Would Betty feel at home there now? Would her theater aspirations be more welcomed or more tolerated today? Odessa is still football country. On Friday, October 10, 2003, 20,000 people watched a high school football game in Ratliff Stadium, a facility that would do most universities proud. The combined OHS-Permian band of around 500 was headed for the 2004 Rose Bowl Parade. Fox Southwest Sports televised the game, a one-point thriller that saw Permian win again on a thirty-six yard field goal against the wind with thirty seconds left in the game. Bissinger would recognize the place, and so did I. What truly intrigued me that day, however, was nothing of what I saw driving around town, at the football game, or in the newspaper. The football game was an after thought because earlier in the day I had rediscovered Betty and her legacy.

"You are related to Betty!" exclaimed the school secretary. Dan and I went to the school to get permission to take pictures in the theater, but being Betty's cousin granted me entrée to so much more. Folks are friendly in Odessa- they really are- but honestly the people at Permian, while welcoming enough to one of their alumni, were frosty compared to OHS. The old school looks great. The teachers seemed bright and friendly towards the students. Dan commented later that a parent would feel comfortable having his child there, even if she were in theater. You can believe that. Dan and I were not just allowed to take pictures. We quickly learned that Betty, or Betty the Ghost, is one of OHS' proudest traditions. Mr. Carl Moore, a veteran high school drama teacher, told us that Betty's legend was one of the first things he learned about OHS when he came there in 2001. Any kid who was late for class or blew a line attributed it to Betty. Noises, cold blasts of air, funny sounds were due to Betty's stirrings.

"There is even a proprietary dispute between athletics and theater about whose ghost she is," said Mr. Moore.

"I can settle that one," I said. "She belongs to the Theater."

"Great," he said, "Would you also like to see the video?"

"Video?" I asked.

"Three students did it in 2001. It's called *In Search of Betty* and it attempts to tell the true story. Of course, you could fill in the blanks," he said.

Dan and I spent a magical afternoon at OHS. We interviewed Mr. Milt Thompson, a teacher/coach, who swears he has seen Betty. He was actually a bit hesitant to talk to me at first and when I gave him the opportunity to read the chapter about the "Ghost of Odessa High," he made sure we all stayed right there while he read it.

"I don't believe in all that ghost stuff, he said, "but I know what I saw and what I felt that morning we came back around 3:30 AM from a baseball tournament in El Paso. Something went down the hall and into a locked door. Fans ran, but they weren't plugged in. A figure glided past the doorway. I saw her." I believe he did.

The kids in Mr. Moore's class knew Betty, too, but they wanted to know more. They were rehearsing a murder mystery, *Blood Money,* and it hurt me to say that I would not be able to come back for it. They absorbed the information in the well-done video, and they soaked up the story I told about *Washed in the Blood.* I wanted to ask them if they were ok, if they could survive in Odessa, Texas, but there was no need. These kids were fine, and they are in excellent hands with Mr. Moore and OHS. They were curious about me though.

"How old were you? They asked.

"Sixteen-she was seventeen," I said.

"Were you close?"

"Very"

"What were you like?"

"I played football."

"Ah we forgive you."

"At Permian."

Giggles and mock horror.

"Sorry, I didn't want to tell you with the big game and all tonight."

An attractive girl sitting on the front row gave a theatrical look around the room. Here sat a whole class of "theater types" at OHS in 2003. What she said made me proud and made me feel great about Betty and my fifteen-year quest. It seemed like such a natural, even obvious comment, but it spoke volumes about their spirit and their sense of self-esteem.

"So, do we look like we care about football?"

Betty would be proud and the kids at OHS are obviously proud and fond of her as well. To Mr. Moore's class and to every kid out there figuring out what it's all about, thanks to you and keep searching. Remember, being from Odessa is no hindrance. Desi, you can be a movie director. Madison, you can be an actor. "Tech guys," you make it all happen. All the rest of you, break a leg, and you are right. If Betty had lived, she might have been your teacher. I can assure you one thing. She is smiling tonight.

Theater Class at OHS, 2003

CHAPTER XXVIX
Three Women

Writing *Washed in the Blood* was not easy. Most of my family did not even want me to do it. I started and stopped a half dozen times. Some people refused to discuss it with me during the research and some who did talk about it with me or with Mark David later disavowed the project. One prominent person important to the story told me not to write it, reviewed the draft, told me that it was an important story that had to be told for all young women, and then blasted it and me after it came out. Frankly, it is about what I expected. What I didn't quite expect is the outpouring of support and appreciation I got from men and women all over the country as a result of the book's publication. Betty did indeed affect the lives of hundreds of people, and, for reasons I will explain below, she will continue to do so for many years to come.

Even though I disliked linking this book to *Friday Night Lights*, the original publisher and I decided to release *Washed in the Blood* at the same time as the movie *Friday Night Lights* came out. Shortly after the movie appeared, Texas Monthly published an article about a massage parlor/house of ill repute that prominent Odessans had frequented. When I was asked to speak to the Odessa

Rotary Club in January 2005, I told them that I wrote *Washed in the Blood* because with *Friday Night Lights* and Texas Monthly, I felt Odessa just wasn't getting enough publicity! Of course I had no idea that in the next year alone, ABC would announce a TV series based on *Friday Night Lights;* that in February "Texas Monthly" would publish a long article about Betty entitled "A Kiss Before Dying"; and that Hollywood would come knocking on my door. Men relate to the story, especially to the aspects dealing with fathers and football, but countless women tell me that they "see themselves" in Betty. These are not all women from the Bible Belt; they are not all in the dramatic arts; and they sure as hell aren't damaged goods. They are bright, thoughtful, and deeply caring human beings. A conservative estimate is that I have heard from around two dozen of these good people. Thanks to each and every one, male and female, who has reached out to me after the publication of *Washed in the Blood.* Folks have asked me if writing the book brought me any closure about the incident. No it didn't. Perhaps a movie will, but it doesn't matter. I am terribly gratified that others have said that the story helped them or helped them counsel young people. You see, a lot of the people who contacted me were high school counselors of some sort who told me that they meet many Bettys every week. My book, I am told, has given them a device for initiating a conversation with a young person about problems, choices, and the ever-lasting permanence of suicide. That is surely one of the consequences for which I aspired as I began to write.

Another, honestly, was to visit with Betty once again. She was such a presence. For many decades I thought I was seeing Betty through a haze of rose-colored nostalgia. The court proceedings made her into a different person—a sad, despondent, weird person—and who she really was seemed lost forever. Slowly, over time, a more balanced view of Betty is coming into view. While Betty is in clearer focus, who she was is not any less complicated. Betty was different in different contexts. I suppose that is true of most of us, but Betty appeared to be a wholly different person depending on where and with whom she was. A pious Sunday School teacher. A wild, hip Beat. A nondescript and shy high school student. A dynamic and effervescent drama student. An obedient child. A tempting vixen. Who did you want her to be? What did you expect her to act like? You name it and Ms. Betty Chameleon would accommodate it. The Betty I knew was only part of who Betty was. To those in her church or who are part of her family, the Betty you knew was real, but there was more to her than you knew. I think that is why Betty and Betty's story are so broadly appealing. We can all find part of ourselves in it.

That is why my recollections of the "Kiss and Kill" incident can only go so far. I can only write of my impressions and my Betty. Others find and emphasize their own truths, and I am more than happy to share their "takes" on it as well. The most important of these began with a phone call in the summer of 2005. A former student of mine at Austin College had read *Washed in the Blood*, lived in Austin, and knew a writer at "Texas Monthly," Pamela Colloff. "Pam Colloff," said Monica Walters, "You need to call Shelly Williams." She did. Pamela had read the book and, like me, became obsessed with the story. How could this have happened? Who were these people? What kind of town was Odessa? Pam did not condemn Odessa for Betty's death. Odessa did not kill Betty in any way, shape or form. But, it is, like Betty or Mack or me, a "character" in the story. Pam later told me that she was totally fascinated by the articulate, lively, and well educated people that grew up in Odessa and had lots to say about the event. She also told me that in fifteen years of writing about true crime in Texas for Texas' "National Magazine," she had never had more people tell her *not* to write a story. Why would a magazine of the stature of Texas Monthly "stoop" to revisit this story and traumatize the survivors once again? That was a frequently heard prior-to-publication complaint. In other words, this story still jangles raw nerves and its reverberations are still expanding. Why? The story has often been retold in the local newspaper. The Ghost of Odessa High School has been sited and discussed for going on three decades. When Warren Burnett died in 2002, numerous authors wrote about his role in the event. What is different about *Washed in the Blood* or Pam's Texas Monthly piece, *A Kiss Before Dying*? Maybe it's because they try to tell the victim's story. It's just a thought.

Read *A Kiss Before Dying*. I don't like that the editors called Betty a "fast girl from the wrong side of the tracks." That's the editor's Betty. I don't agree with one or two of the sequencing of events the article presents, but in truth, it is a wonderful piece of journalism. Pam found people I could not find, Dick Bowles principally. She dug up information that I had only guessed at: Betty did in fact have a diary. She presents the story in a straight-line narrative that *Washed in the Blood* intentionally avoids. (It is my impressionistic retelling after all.) Most importantly, she confirms both the broad outlines and most of the details of *Washed in the Blood*. As I wrote the book, some people challenged the details. The play, they recalled, was *Of Mice and Men,* not *Winterset*. Betty had not been the stage manager of the play; she was just around. My former girl friend didn't recall that I had been at the July 4th party, that we had broken up over my wanting to leave, or that we didn't date during our senior years! Surely, Shell, the town didn't divide for and against Mack as you say. Pam found and confirmed the truth of all of this. Hard work and research often trump memory.

I discovered this to be true on my most recent trip to Odessa, in October, 2006.

The journey back to Odessa was amazing and disturbing. The best part was finding the stock pond where Betty died and then going back last night at 10:00 PM to drive the highway they took out there. We climbed the fence and then walked the road that Betty and Mack drove. We used flashlights. The pond looked like a Hollywood set and the West Texas sky was in full glory. Bright stars, arranged in spectacular formations, just for us. Wisps of clouds on loan from a John Ford movie. Eight vertical red pillars standing at the break in the horizon meant for the movie but guiding small planes into the county airport in the meantime. A picked-apart coyote carcass lay at the very spot Betty died and the stench of death lingered through our two visits to the pond. The professionals who were with me took multiple images that may some day strike lots of folks as beautiful. I fought back tears and thanked God that Betty's last view was a spectacular one.

Most importantly, we met a lot of people. The kids at OHS were even more energetic and engaging than the last visit in 2003. Everywhere we went, people told me how great *Washed in the Blood* was, how much they learned about Odessa, and how great an impact it had on their lives. Then we met a retired teacher, the woman I knew Betty loved and who I thought had been her drama teacher. She early on indicated that she was not excited about meeting me, but for some foolish reason I wanted to meet her. She is elderly; she wears poorly coordinated clothes; and her memory is highly selective because she remembers wonderful details of long-ago speech tournaments, class assignments, and personalities, but she blanks on the most infamous event that occurred during her tenure at OHS.

"Do you remember Betty Williams?" I asked.

"No, I really don't," she replied.

"Well," I said, "she really loved you."

"That's what I understand."

We were in the lobby of the McM Grande Hotel on the eastern outskirts of Odessa. The teacher sat in the overstuffed chair and one of her former students sat on the couch next to her. A movie producer sat directly across from her and I knelt on one knee to her side, my hand sharing the armrest. I waited an eternity of seconds to see if she would say anything more about the girl, but she was finished. Later, to the producer, she would acknowledge that she had received a copy of my book from her enthusiastic son. It was clear she had not read it because she later asked me what school I had attended "back then." She had no comment when I said Permian. Maybe she felt a tinge of embarrassment at the moment, but probably not. She had earlier dismissed Permian as "Premium High." She had bragged (there is no other word) that "back then" OHS had been THE school, that her speech program had been the best in the state, that the principal's job at OHS was the most prestigious educational position in town, that she had been dean at the Junior College and that there were not one but two PhDs in her family. Before her sat a former student she had not seen in forty-two years, a movie producer, and an author. In my presence she asked not a single meaningful question of any of us. When told that the group had visited OHS the day before and had met an amazing group of theater students and a talented and caring new drama teacher, she said that then we had, of course, seen the plaque at the school dedicated to her accomplishments.

Not long into the visit, I removed myself from her side and I sunk into the thick pillows on the couch. I made pleasant comments for a few minutes but soon I sat there in stony silence. I cannot have a grudge against someone with poor memory or someone with pride in genuine accomplishments. She didn't have to like Betty the way Betty loved her. She even had the option to see her former student without seeing me. That she chose to visit me is a mystery. That she ever taught my sensitive, loving, confused cousin is a shame.

What helped with my own memory when I went to work on this edition of the book and what is amazing about Pam's journalism is that she found a lot more than she could publish and then even more turned up after her story appeared. In the former category, consider Life Magazine. In the early '60s, Life was *the* magazine in the US. I had long been aware that Life had someone there to take pictures at the Beaumont trial, but I had never known that it and one of its writers had completed a story about the event. And even had I assumed that it had written a story, I had no idea it would still be around. Pam found it. There is no explanation why Life didn't publish it. Perhaps other events were more compelling. Maybe it was not up to Life's standards. Who knows? What we do know is that the only surviving evidence of Life's presence are Shel

Hershorn's brilliant images (now done justice in this edition) and Life's selection of Warren Burnett as one of 1963's "Top 100 Young Men in America." The Life piece did help point Pam's research (and mine) in certain directions and it helped clarify some aspects of the case. It was also solid confirmation that Pam and I weren't alone in considering the "Kiss and Kill" Murder a matter of national importance. One can only speculate what the impact would have been in 1962 if Life had printed the story.

In terms of impact, Gayle Guffey Ross, the former OHS student mentioned above, can provide great detail about how the incident affected her. Neither Pam nor I had the benefit of her insights when we wrote our stories. I did know about Gayle Guffey when I was writing, and she is represented by several persons in the book. Most prominently, she is Annabelle, Betty's best friend. She is also the person who went on to perform opera in Denver. Mark David had interviewed her in 1986 and I had known about her in 1962. Some of it we got wrong. Gayle didn't quit acting class and she didn't share Betty's feelings about the teacher. She had great talent, but she never made diva status in Denver. She was never a cheerleader. The rest Pam and I got just about right. After Gayle read Pam's article, she wrote to me at Austin College. I had already left Sherman, Texas for Washington, DC. It took me two months to get her long letter, but it was worth waiting for. Gayle's Betty was my Betty. Gayle knew of her energy, talent, relationships, hopes and aspirations. They planned to go to Indiana University together. She also knew that Betty was not totally obsessed and hooked on Mack so much that she wanted to die. How? Mack was dating Gayle and Betty knew it. Mack kissed Gayle good-bye, left her house to get gas for his jeep, and then went to Betty's to pick her up the night Betty died. Gayle's opinion is the same as mine: Betty didn't intend to die. She was being dramatic to get Mack's attention.

It is important to note that while I knew about Gayle, she had no idea that I even existed. She knew that Mark was to write a book, but she didn't know his writing partner and when his book never appeared, she gave up hope. She found out about me and *Washed in the Blood* almost by accident as she flipped through the February 2006 edition of Texas Monthly. Her letter to me (which I print in part below with her permission) is a powerful statement of how the Kiss and Kill Murder affected one life. In a curious way, Betty, Gayle and Pam have become part of a woman's story. Three women. I will let Gayle have the last word.

CHAPTER XXX
From a Friend

February 5, 2006

Dear Shelly:

 I feel as though I know you, although we've only met through the pages of your book, "Washed in the Blood." It arrived Friday night and I finished reading it Saturday morning. I ordered it online immediately after reading the article in "Texas Monthly."

 I knew Betty. I knew Mack. I was close to the murder and the events, even though you may not have heard of me.

 Back in 1961 my name was Gayle Guffey. I had the female lead in "Winterset," the role of Miriamne. That's when I got to know Betty—during play rehearsals and the drama department. I am the "Gayle" Betty referred to in one of her last notes: "Gayle, I'm sorry about Indiana." Betty and I formed one of those intense, dramatic friendships that teenage girls (and drama queens) form so easily. She was a senior; I was a sophomore. We became close friends in the few months before her murder. I considered her my best friend at the time. Don't know if she felt the same, but she said she did. She called

173

me her best friend. But as you so accurately pointed out, Betty was vivid, dramatic, bursting at the seams with life—she probably had a whole host of best friends I wasn't aware of. She knew far more people than I did, and she had far more friends than I did. In a way, I clung to that close, intense relationship with Betty, and suspect because of my youth and awkwardness and lack of social skills, I needed her friendship in those months far more than she needed mine. As I remember it, I spent the one of the last nights of her life in her room at her house, talking, laughing, fantasizing about our future as roommates at Indiana University, starring together in all the productions. I spent many such evenings at her house.

One of my most vivid memories of Betty is how she smelled of "Here's My Heart" perfume (Avon). I could never tolerate that scent again after she died.

I got to know Mack as a result of "Winterset," and he and I dated a few times. Before Winterset, I only knew him from a distance—we were not in the same social circles. He was a football player, and a popular guy, and like Betty I loathed football and that whole football frenzy. When Mack and I "dated," he didn't take me out in public either (just like Betty). I always figured that was because I was chubby, not a bit pretty, and was known as an "egghead—too smart." None of the popular boys wanted to be seen dating smart girls. Mack, of course, was really just sneaking around seeing different girls on the sly, while he pursued his on-and-off-again relationship with Sherry Martin. But I was so out of the OHS social loop, I didn't know any of that at the time.

The afternoon before Mack murdered Betty, Dick Bowles, Enid Woodward and I had gone out to KMID Channel 2 television to participate in a late afternoon talk show, perform a couple of brief scenes from "Winterset" and promote the play. Then we all met at OHS for a short, late rehearsal. Afterward, probably about 8:30 or 9:00, Mack drove me home as he frequently did after rehearsal. We sat in the driveway talking for a few minutes; then he said he had to leave to put gas in his jeep before he went home. He kissed me goodnight and drove off.

I guess he did need gas, with that long drive ahead of him to Winkler County.

I knew about Betty's broken relationship with Mack. I knew about her brief relationship with Will Rosebud. I do not recognize the girl you call Annabelle Jackson in the book, but would love to know who this is, if it doesn't violate confidentiality.

I met Betty's parents, and at the time I thought the family dynamics were so bizarre as to be frightening. Forget about the hyper-religiosity—that was just a sanctimonious ruse. All the behaviors and the dynamics in that family—Betty's promiscuity, his hyper-vigilance, her mother's passivity—all are, to me, consistent with a bizarre, unwholesome constellation of relationships.

The following morning (Mack had murdered Betty only a few hours earlier), I got a phone call about 7:00 a.m. from Mrs. Williams. Betty was not in her room, and it looked like she hadn't been there all night. Did I know where she was? I assured her I didn't, but secretly I suspected she had snuck off to spend the night with a radio disk jockey she recently claimed to have been sleeping with. I didn't tell her mother that, of course, but instead reassured her that I thought everything was okay. I also thought that Betty sure was going to be in major trouble when her parents found her.

I immediately phoned Mack! I told him about the call from Mrs. Williams and asked him if he knew where Betty was! He said he didn't, but he was sure "she would turn up."

Of course I knew nothing about what had happened the previous night. Later I remembered how ordinary Mack sounded during that early morning phone call. If anything, he seemed detached or "flat," but I thought I'd just awakened him and he was tired and sleepy. Today, at 61, I would realize he was not normal— the flat emotional affect was shock or sociopathy or dissociation. Back then, I didn't know enough about people to decipher what I was hearing.

I went to school that morning. Betty's parents filed a missing person's report, and the police pulled me out of first period geometry class and questioned me for about thirty minutes. My recollection from that moment on is the school buzzing, crackling with gossip. I checked at the office repeatedly to see if they had any new information. I also remember the shock and outrage classmates displayed when Mack was interviewed and then left school with the police. When I went to the office shortly after noon, they suggested I call my mother and go home. They already knew something terrible had happened.

Mother picked me up but instead of taking me home, immediately took me "shopping for an Easter dress." She wouldn't let me turn on the radio. Of course she was keeping me occupied and away from newscasts. When we returned home at 4:00, my father's car was there and I knew immediately something was terribly wrong. My father was like a clock—he always got home between 5:15 and 5:30, and his routine never varied.

I ran into the house and asked "Did they find Betty?" Father said, "Yes." I said, "Is she okay?" He said something like "She is dead." I said, "What happened?" He said, "Mack shot her."

At that point I collapsed, not believing. I couldn't stop crying. I will never forget crying and crying for hours—so much that my pillow was soaked with tears. I couldn't stop. The upheaval was so profound I started my period two weeks early. I was in shock.

I don't think I was "normal" after that for years. I went into what I now know was a dissociative state. I walked through my life, not fully inhabiting my body—observing myself from a distance far above my head. I remember my high school and college years like this.

Within days of Betty's murder I started sleeping to escape—12-14 hours a day. My parents didn't know what to do, but they sure didn't want any mention of the murder in the house. We had a screaming match about the funeral—they didn't want me to go. I insisted. I went with friends because my parents refused to take me or accompany me. All they wanted was their life back, the way it was "before."

176

They didn't "believe in" psychotherapy; the only counseling they allowed was sending me to Fr. Berry at St. John's Episcopal Church, where we were parishioners. That was another terrible experience for me on the heels of the murder. Fr. Berry took the attitude that just knowing Betty and Mack meant I was an awful, sinful person, and the misery I felt was because I didn't have a good relationship with Jesus!

I severed ties with religion then and there.

I, too, went to see Mack after the murder. In the dreadful first weeks "after," I couldn't accept that this boy, someone I really liked and thought I knew, could do this horrible thing. But I only went to see him once. I must have grasped the unseemliness of talking to him. Logic prevailed. I realized that, bottom line, no one and nothing compelled him to pull that trigger. When I went to see him that one time I thought I saw shame and confusion in his demeanor and affect, but I believed then and now that Mack created this tragedy by his actions and his actions were always under his control.

Mack acted, but all Betty did was talk. Asking people to kill her was nothing but a pathetic, melodramatic stunt on her part. She never believed anyone would take her seriously. Maybe she thought she could manipulate Mack into feeling so sorry for her he would have an epiphany—"Oh God! What have I done to this wonderful, unique girl. I've been a fool."

And they would ride off into the sunset together instead of driving to a stock pond in the middle of the night.

It was certainly a bluff on her part. Her comments to Ike Nail when Mack drove up proved that. I believe they both had written mental scripts about how this scene would play out. I always believed Mack's script was "I'll teach her a lesson. She will be so scared at how close we came to doing this, she will grow up and stop the dramatic crap." Betty's script was, "When Mack sees how miserable I am, and how much I love him, he will realize that we should be together, and he will take me back."

Betty's fatal miscalculation was misreading Mack.

Something terribly flawed in him let him step right to the line on this bluff and then actually pull the trigger before they could play out their mental scripts. (On one level I was also furious with Betty for playing such a manipulative, melodramatic game with people's lives and emotions. If Betty didn't really want to die, didn't really intend to carry this out, there is no other possible conclusion than that she played a manipulative, attention-seeking game.)

On the other hand, there is the damning evidence of the weights and the wire. I always asked myself why Mack went prepared to hide her body if it was just a bluff on his part. Was this to show Betty he would go through with it, to scare her into backing down quickly? Or was he intent on killing her? I don't know, and no one does except Mack himself. All I know is that it altered dozens of lives afterwards.

They were both foolish, dangerous, stupid kids playing with fire.

I was called to the police station for several depositions. The prosecution put me under subpoena. I sure wasn't one of "Mack's girls" and I openly spoke out against him. The groupie mentality that surrounded and "supported" Mack and made him a kind of celebrity following the murder was incomprehensible to me. It seemed to me that I was almost shunned by many people at school.

I heard a rumor that some classmates believed I knew something that would send Mack to the electric chair. What drivel! All I was trying to do was survive and make sense of the incomprehensible. I could barely function, and though I didn't realize it at the time, I began having panic attacks that recurred during times of stress for more than ten years. At one point during my college years I was virtually agoraphobic with panic. And in college I drank heavily.

Would all that have happened if not for Betty and Mack? Who can say? But certainly the murder and its aftermath triggered a constellation of problems coping with stress that took years to work through and recover from.

A word about Enid Woodward. I never knew Betty hated her; she never told me that. I was a sophomore in 1961—fresh out of Bowie Junior High. It was my first year at OHS. I cannot address Betty's acting talent as I never saw her perform. Enid Woodward probably wasn't a good teacher—as I remember this was a stop-gap job for her, not a career choice—but she was an absolute life-saver to me. Maybe she was cold and harsh with Betty, but Mrs. Woodward was loving and kind to me. In fact, she probably realized more than anyone how lost I was.

I was dangerously depressed after the murder. I sought Mrs. Woodward out one afternoon, in utter misery—even contemplating suicide. She wrapped her arms around me and hugged me and brushed back my hair and held my face in her hands. She told me I was wonderful and strong and to hold my head up and ignore all the stupid people who were being unkind. Those words stayed with me through many difficult times. The following summer, she hired me to watch her little girl during the summer. That routine, which forced me to be active and not just hide at home, helped me function instead of withdraw further.

Years later, when I entered psychotherapy, my therapist said it was a miracle I didn't have a psychotic break during this time. I believe that is true, and I think Enid Woodward, more than anyone, helped me through this time.

I'm not discounting what Betty told you, or arguing with her belief. I'm just saying there was much more to Enid Woodward than Betty's opinion of her. Mrs. Woodward went through her own hell as a result of Mack and Betty's actions, and who is to say how hard it was for her to cope? Every decision she had made that school year, every word she had uttered, was surely scrutinized and second-guessed, and I'm sure she was held (and felt?) partially responsible for the tragic events, which really were none of her doing. She was as caught up and victimized by their actions as we all were.

Later, in college, I finally stopped thinking about Betty and Mack. I erased the murder from my mind for almost twenty years. I *majored in music, sang professionally on a minor scale for years. Objectively, I probably had the talent for a major career in opera. But I believe I didn't pursue that as actively as I could have because of the effect the murder had on me. Very much like you described for yourself, I sought a level of safety and security, a life I could control and manage and protect, because life had spun so out of control in 1961. I married and divorced twice, but managed to get one wonderful daughter out of that.*

All those memories came back in the late 1980's when I was contacted in Denver (where I lived for 30 years) by Mark David who was researching a book about Betty and Mack. He flew in and we spent hours going over the murder. I drank heavily that night, having all those memories revisited, and I could not have been much help. Poor guy must have found it a total waste of time.

Now, in 2006, I have a life that I love on many levels, even though it was tough getting from there to here. I am a grandmother and have a great relationship with my daughter and son-in-law and little grandson and granddaughter. I relocated to Plano, Texas in late 2003. I have a supervisory job with the Plano police department, and have made many new friends.

Several years ago I fulfilled a life-long dream. I took nine months off and traveled solo around the world with just a backpack. Last December I took another overseas trip, spending a month in Eastern Europe. Now I give travel and motivational lectures here in the Dallas area, and that fulfilling activity is expanding, perhaps into a new direction for my life.

Thanks to years of intense therapy, I think I am now reasonably mentally healthy. But a good thirty years of my life were spent careening around on a level of dysfunction that bordered on craziness—certainly foolishness. I was lucky (and hard-working) enough to make it to the other side.

Control remains a huge issue for me. Complete independence, rejecting the need for other people, avoiding vulnerability, may be my most defining character traits today. Home is not just where I am comfortable, it is also my private, unique, safe territory. I try to avoid controlling others (impossible anyway), but I become irritable, almost panicked if I think someone or some thing is controlling my life. I've learned to accept and cope with those feelings constructively, but they still return and are still unsettling. I continue to struggle with occasional bouts of depression. Would I be this way if it hadn't been for Betty and Mack and the events of March 1961? Maybe--perhaps this would have been my fundamental personality no matter what. Or maybe not. I am sure of only one thing--that those events influenced me in ways I may still not recognize.

All things considered, I probably turned out pretty darn well.

Well, that is my story, and what happened to me after the murder. Thought you might be interested in how it affected another minor player in the event.

I thought your book was terrific. Thank you for writing it. I loved the descriptions of life in Odessa in the '60s And thanks for writing it from Betty's perspective. The victims are rarely heard from.

All of us were victims. Betty may have been the one murdered, but the circumstances of her death caused other deaths—the death of dreams, hopes, trust, security, even believing the world was comprehensible and manageable.

Those of us who lived through those times lost much more than just Betty.

Note: If you would like to share this letter with anyone, please do so.

A Betty X Production

WASHED IN THE BLOOD
(John Williams, 2004)

"Do we look like we care about football at all?"
That's what the drama girls say.
They put me in mind of an old friend of mine
Who was sure that the thing was the play.
She played major roles and she stole every show
And she glowed in the theater lights.
But it came crashing down on the outskirts of town
In the dark of a West Texas night.

At age seventeen, she bought cheap gasoline
And she ran with those wild Texas boys.
Then—sudden one day—all the parts went away
And she wound up confused and annoyed.
She started to talk about ending it all
But none of us thought that she would.
'Til she found a young man who bought into the plan
And he ended her troubles for good

      Alone in a world she could not recognize
      Where nothing made sense but the tears in her eyes.
      She lived in the spotlight and died in the mud,
      Finally washed in the blood.

We put on our ties and we polished our lies
And went down to the church by the square
Solemn and grim, we all sang bloody hymns
And tried hard not to see what was there.
Did she pay the price of supreme sacrifice
So that some girls can be who they are?
Or was it in fact just the bad final act
Of a high school theatrical star?

No one was sure what was illness or cure,
What were cheap lies and what were the facts.
It was all said and done when he fired that gun
Now she's gone and she's not coming back
The judge called his name; said, "Son, you're not to blame
You just did what she told you to do."
But what kind of world says you can shoot a girl
Even if she asks you to?
What kind of world says you can shoot a girl
Even if she asks you to?

    Alone in a world she could not recognize
    Where nothing made sense but the tears in her eyes.
    She lived in the spotlight and died in the mud,
    Finally washed in the blood.

"Do we look like we care about football at all?"
That's what the drama girls say.

Printed in the United States
205227BV00005B/148-183/A